Praise for
Jud Wilhite

"*Torn* is a combination of honesty, insight, and biblical wisdom. Jud Wilhite is as transparent as he is encouraging and as truthful as he is wise."

—ANDY STANLEY, senior pastor of North Point
Community Church

"In *Torn,* Jud Wilhite demonstrates how God's Word, taught simply and lovingly, transforms lives."

—RICK WARREN, author of *The Purpose Driven Life*
and founding pastor of Saddleback Church

"In *Torn,* Jud puts his heart on the line for readers who are suffering. Then he gently leads them into a healing encounter with a God who can be trusted in every circumstance. If you feel torn, I highly recommend this book!"

—MARK BATTERSON, author of *In a Pit with a Lion
on a Snowy Day* and lead pastor of National
Community Church

"*Torn* speaks straight to the heart with profound biblical encouragement for the stuff we all face. This book doesn't offer easy answers but a powerful, needed message of hope for weary travelers."

—STEVEN FURTICK, author of *Sun Stand Still*
and lead pastor of Elevation Church

"In *Torn*, Jud Wilhite takes you beyond the why questions of suffering to challenge you with what it means to trust God in everything. He stretches your faith and offers real insight to help you move forward and cling to God."

—PETE WILSON, author of *Plan B* and founding and senior pastor of Cross Point Church

"*Torn* is like a cold drink of water in the dry desert of difficulties. Jud writes with great compassion, wisdom, and humor to show us how God uses the tough times to shape us."

—PERRY NOBLE, founding and senior pastor of NewSpring Church

"What God is up to in Vegas is nothing short of hard-core. Jud describes an extreme faith that is extremely amazing. With clarity and passion, *Uncensored Grace* offers a renewed sense of hope for whatever you are up against. Don't miss this book."

—STEPHEN BALDWIN, actor and author of *The Unusual Suspect*

"Jud Wilhite is a compelling new voice and model for a new way to be Christian in today's culture."

—GABE LYONS, author of *The Next Christians*

"*Stripped* is full of surprises and twists. It will captivate and inspire you as it describes the difference Jesus can make in your life."

—LEE STROBEL, author of *The Case for Christ*

TORN

TORN

Trusting God When Life Leaves You in Pieces

JUD WILHITE

MULTNOMAH
BOOKS

Torn
Published by Multnomah Books
12265 Oracle Boulevard, Suite 200
Colorado Springs, Colorado 80921

Details in some anecdotes and stories have been changed to protect the identities of the persons involved.

ISBN 978-1-60142-073-2
ISBN 978-1-60142-303-0 (electronic)

Cover design by Tim Green, Faceout Studio.

Published in association with Yates & Yates, LLP, Attorneys and Counselors, Orange, California.

Published in the United States by WaterBrook Multnomah, an imprint of the Crown Publishing Group, a division of Random House Inc., New York.

Multnomah and its mountain colophon are registered trademarks of Random House Inc.

Library of Congress Cataloging-in-Publication Data
Wilhite, Jud, 1971-
   Torn : trusting God when life leaves you in pieces / Jud Wilhite. — 1st ed.
      p. cm.
   Includes bibliographical references (p.   ).
   ISBN 978-1-60142-073-2 — ISBN 978-1-60142-303-0 (electronic)
   1. Suffering—Religious aspects—Christianity. 2. Trust in God—Christianity. I. Title.
BV4909.W535 2011
248.8'6—dc22
                                    2011006716

Printed in the United States of America
2011

10 9 8 7 6 5 4 3 2

Special Sales
Most WaterBrook Multnomah books are available at special quantity discounts when purchased in bulk by corporations, organizations, and special-interest groups. Custom imprinting or excerpting can also be done to fit special needs. For information, please e-mail SpecialMarkets@WaterBrook Multnomah.com or call 1-800-603-7051.

To the leadership team at Central,
servants with a heart for those who are torn

CONTENTS

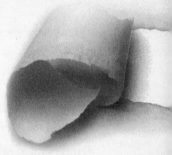

Introduction

I'm naturally a joyful person who has been accused of smiling too much—an accusation I hope people will toss my way the rest of my life. But I had entered a season when the smile was all but gone. I felt like Bilbo Baggins in *The Fellowship of the Ring* when he said, "I'm old, Gandalf. I know I don't look it, but I'm beginning to feel it in my heart. I feel...thin. Sort of stretched, like...butter scraped over too much bread."[1]

We had experienced years of remarkable expansion in the church I served, and I felt like I was always running as hard as I could to keep up. As growth surged, we also found ourselves in a deep local recession. Navigating cutbacks, counseling a sea of individuals and friends who were reduced to desperation, and leading with no compass for unprecedented times began to take its toll. I've traveled enough to know that Western poverty and global poverty are very different things, yet the pain of this economic struggle was profound and surprising. The number of suicides in our community and our church testified to the reality of the despair.

And then there were more personal struggles. I watched emphysema steal my mom's capacity to breathe and eventually take her life. While grieving her loss, I found myself attacked and mischaracterized by bloggers, some of whom knew almost nothing about me. I topped off the season with a visit to see how my father was holding up after Mom's death. When I got there, I found he had just been taken to the hospital, his own health deteriorating.

As the trials mounted, I found myself wondering why. All this stuff hitting me at the same time just didn't seem fair. Of course, I knew my difficulties didn't compare with the hardships that many face, but they were mine (just as yours are yours), and tough is tough. Perspective provides only so much consolation before it stops providing consolation altogether. One day I found myself sitting with my face in my hands, feeling a weird mix of emptiness and heaviness. Sort of a collision between blah and *arggh*! It felt like my world was ripping apart.

Can you relate? Have you ever wondered where God is in the mess of life? Have you ever felt like something that happened to you just wasn't fair?

Have you ever felt *torn*?

It's Not Fair!

The sense that things aren't fair ricochets around our planet every second of every day, not least of all around my own home. My daughter, Emma, will say of her brother, "Ethan picked the movie last week, and if he gets to pick again, it's not fair!"

I'll hear, "Emma had two chocolates earlier, and if I don't get another, it's not fair."

I'll say, "I took out the trash last time. It's Mom's turn, or it's not fair!" (Okay, I don't have the guts to say this, but I do think it.)

Everyone knows what it feels like to get the short end of the stick. Your neighbor pulls up in a shiny new car while you drive a beater. Your slacker friend at work gets a raise while you scrape by. Your spouse gets cancer while you're each in your prime. Your teenager starts using drugs. Your child is diagnosed with an incurable condition. Your husband is killed on the battlefield. Your desire for alcohol drowns out everything you love. Your life swirls down the toilet. It's not fair. Even the biblical Job got in the act when he said, "God has no right to treat me like this—it isn't fair!"[2]

> Everyone knows what it feels like to get the short end of the stick.

We're torn. We suffer. We struggle. And we wonder why.

We shout, shout, let it all out. (And, yes, along with Tears for Fears, these are things I can do without.)

STARTING AT *WHY*

Sometimes, in the midst of it all, we are tempted to doubt God's goodness—or at least his goodness to *us*. Sure, he may be a good God, we think, but obviously we're receiving some sort of payback for the wrongs we've done or for the good things we've left undone. Perhaps God is getting even with us for a botched marriage, our mediocre parenting, or the abortion we never told anyone about.

We search for a reason. *If God really loves me and cares for me, then why is this happening? If he is good, then why doesn't he step in and make things right? Why doesn't he ride up on a white horse and fix this mess?*

Then we look at the larger world and wonder, *Why doesn't he stop the tsunami before it rolls over thousands of men, women, and children? Why doesn't he prevent the tornado from plowing through a home filled with good people? Why doesn't he stop earthquakes and mud slides and falling bridges? Or terrorist attacks and child abuse and drunk drivers?*

When unexpected and incomprehensible things like these happen, we're also tempted to doubt God's power. *Maybe,* we think, *he just isn't mighty enough to make a differ-*

ence. *Perhaps he's doing his best in this broken world, but there is only so much he can do.* This train of thought certainly keeps God's goodness intact, but it isn't very comforting when the next crisis comes.

Some of us turn from the faith altogether. Bart Ehrman became a self-described born-again Christian as a teenager and eventually became a professor of religious studies. But he lost his faith along the way. He's written a book titled *God's Problem: How the Bible Fails to Answer Our Most Important Question—Why We Suffer.* Ehrman said, "I could no longer reconcile the claims of faith with the facts of life.... I came to the point where I simply could not believe that there is a good and kindly disposed Ruler who is in charge."[3] Yet to me his answer raises even more questions. To go Ehrman's route is to affirm my loneliness and confusion, leaving me adrift in a universe with no hope.

Such perspectives are not new. There have been countless books and debates on the issue of God and evil, enough to fill entire libraries. Still, the fact remains that you suffer. I suffer. We all suffer. And our reflex to pain and suffering is to ask why.

As I turned to the Bible in my pain, I was surprised to discover that God's response to this question is unlike anything the philosophers or I would expect. In fact, he gives us a new question.

Moving On to *Who*

When it comes to evil and suffering, the Bible refuses to answer why. It simply and powerfully upholds the validity of the question! We read of a God who is sovereign and good, all-powerful and all-loving. He's strong enough to end our suffering and perfect enough in his goodness to desire the best for us. Yet there is no airtight resolution to the perpetual earthly drama of suffering.

But there is so much more.

We learn in the Bible that God turns our suffering to good, that he trades it for joy later on, that it makes us more like Christ, that it allows his glory to be known in our lives, and that it is an encouragement to trust him (because if everything were perfect all the time, why would we need faith?). But these aren't the answers we're going for when we're torn.

So the testimonies of the Bible about pain and suffering and the consequences of sin are not mathematical formulas for rational understanding. Instead they are constant proclamations about the God who rules and loves, and they are constant reminders to cast our cares on him. God wants us to hope in *him*.

In other words, *why* is not the most fundamental human question when it comes to suffering. Even if we had all the answers to our whys, we might actually find them unsatisfying and ultimately unredemptive for the pain we are facing. A bigger question emerges.

The most fundamental question, according to the Bible, is *who*. Who will we trust in the calamities and challenges of life? Who will we turn to in the reality of our pain? *Who is worthy of our trust?*

In my recent emotional and spiritual challenges, the trustworthiness of God's character gave me hope. By adjusting my focus from the circumstances in my life to the awesome sovereignty of God, I began to delight in him in deeper and richer ways. I matured. Difficulty has a way of doing that; it grows us up and prepares us for the next phase God has for us.

> *Why* is not the most fundamental question when it comes to suffering. The most fundamental question is *who*. Who will we trust in the calamities of life?

When the world comes crashing down, all at once or a bit at a time, it does damage to more than our peace; it shakes our assurance, our security, our faith. Something inside us tears. Yet God is near to us when we are torn up, mending the frayed edges of our hearts.

In fact, what we find is that pain doesn't rule out an all-powerful and loving God so much as an all-powerful and loving God rules over pain. Even if you get the *why* question answered, it's not likely to make the pain of losing a loved one or the difficulty in finding work suddenly go away. But if we know who is mighty to save and loving enough to do it in ways we usually don't expect, we can see our pain and suffering in a new light. And then we can go on to deal with it in the here and now.

And Finally...*How*?

Most people I counsel are eager to see their pain and suffering differently. Often they are desperate for anything that will help them sort out their thoughts and feelings, because the chaos of their circumstances makes them feel as if they're drowning. It's fine to proclaim God's goodness and grace, to assure each other of his sovereign control over our torn lives and broken hearts. We can talk for miles about the right road. But believing the car will go means nothing until we put it into Drive.

After *who,* we want to know—we *need* to know—*how.* How do we move on? How do we sort out our thoughts and feelings? How do we gather strength? How do we build on the ruins around us? How do we forgive? How do we make the millions of tiny decisions that add up to a life committed to God even when our heart is broken?

In the following pages I'll share what I've learned as we explore this God who cares and the hope he provides.

We'll start with the *who* question in part 1, looking at

the importance of trusting a God who is powerful and sovereign even when we are torn apart. We'll reflect on what it means to examine our expectations of God and life from a biblical perspective. And we'll see how worthy God is of our trust, not only because he rules, but also because he is good and he loves.

In part 2, we'll broaden things to consider more of the *how* question so we can move forward and put the pieces of our lives back together. We'll see the importance of participating in community and evaluating our assumptions about God and others. We'll discover practical ways to fight for joy and to deal with negative feelings, such as grief, anger, and depression. We'll discuss how to forgive others and how to embrace forgiveness ourselves. We'll reclaim hope and perspective to heal.

If you long for a God who is worthy for who he is, not just for what he gives…

If you need to know that you aren't alone in your pain, that God is good and powerful and *for you*…

If you are tired of half-baked answers and desire a faith with guts that will stand in the difficulties of life…

Then read on. We'll learn to worship a good God even when we are torn, and we'll discover hope for our broken lives.

Part 1

Trusting God
When Torn

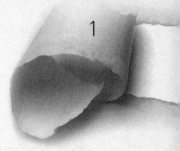

Torn Apart

When I was growing up, the playground was the setting for an entire series of nonsanctioned school games. These games were different from tag and duck, duck, goose. This elite category of games has been handed down from generation to generation. Games like monkey bar wars, truth or dare, and kill the carrier, to name just a few.

One of the most famous nonsanctioned playground games is bloody knuckles. In case you're not familiar with it, let me explain that bloody knuckles is a simple game that tests your speed, your strength, and most important, your tolerance for pain. Two kids stand facing each other with knuckles touching. Then one tries to whack the other's knuckles as hard as he can. Next, the other kid goes. Back and forth, whack after whack. This goes on until one of them quits for a simple reason: the pain becomes too intense.

The game has grown so much in popularity that there is now a World Bloody Knuckles Association (WBKA). The WBKA has a commissioner, official rules, and an option for membership. For just ten dollars, you can receive a membership card and a bumper sticker.[1]

Ever feel like life is one big game of bloody knuckles? Except for one difference—you can't quit. Every time you turn around, you get whacked. You try to dodge it. *Whack!* You beg it to stop. *Whack!* You pray. *Whack!* You do everything in your power to avoid it. *Whack! Whack! Whack!* The pain intensifies. The suffering is daunting. And you're not sure what to do with it or where God is in it.

Maybe you recently experienced your own version of bloody knuckles. Maybe you lost a loved one, and the hurt has turned to denial and anger. You're really confused. Perhaps you lost a job, and the frustration and discouragement continue to grow. You read about God's promises, but you don't understand why this has happened. Maybe you live with chronic pain. You would give anything just to be free of pain and not be distracted by it.

Regardless of your situation, I know that when your very soul is being torn apart, you want an answer for "What am I supposed to do?" And I know from experience that it often feels as though there's nothing you can do. But the primary equipment you need to trust God in your pain and suffering *is* your pain and suffering. You already have the necessary tools; you just need the skilled hands of a loving God to wield them. So the first thing to do at the site of rebuilding is to hand over the tools in trust.

In this chapter we'll consider what it looks like to hand over these tools and worship God in our struggles. Most of us, when faced with enormous obstacles or daunting challenges, like to pull ourselves up by our own bootstraps, trust in our own abilities, and say confidently, "I've got this." But since we have a relationship with the God of the universe, who loves us and cares for us, it makes infinitely more sense to submit to him and say, "God, *you* take this one."

> Most of us, when faced with daunting challenges, say confidently, "I've got this." But it makes infinitely more sense to say, "God, *you* take this one."

DREAM DETOURS

My friends Chris and Kim Trethewey went through several years that felt like one long, losing game of bloody knuckles. About a year and a half into their marriage, they decided to start trying to have kids. The thought of having a family captured their hearts and consumed their conversations. They assumed that in no time they'd have two kids and the white picket fence. They would live the American Dream.

The reality was far from the ideal, and it tore their lives apart. After enduring three and a half years of unsuccessful fertility treatments, they sat down with a doctor who said, "We've done everything we can. We don't know why, but you're not able to have kids."

Chris and Kim walked with an emotional limp after this tremendous blow, but eventually they explored other options. Through an incredible series of events, they adopted two siblings: Kiara, who had just turned one, and Caden, who was three months old.

Caden was born four months premature and was still in the hospital when my friends first saw him. He had been there since birth, with three holes in his heart and under-developed lungs. A devoted medical team repaired his heart and inserted a tracheal tube to help his breathing. Remarkably, his health improved, and the doctors were extremely positive about his future. He began eating regular foods and drinking out of bottles. Time was all that was needed for his lungs to develop.

Chris and Kim virtually lived at the hospital for months until they finally got both kids home. Each day they thanked God for answering their prayers and blessing them with children. Their dream had finally become a reality.

Then one morning around seven o'clock, Caden's apnea

monitor went off. Chris ran in to find Caden in his crib with a distressed look on his face unlike any Chris had seen before. Chris called 911 and tried to give little Caden CPR, but it wasn't working.

Chris remembers, "I'll never lose that image in my mind of just knowing there was nothing I could do. I begged God. I begged him for a miracle. I begged God to save his life. I sat there, and I said everything I could to say, 'God, please! I've seen you work miracle after miracle in the lives of so many people. Today I need you to save my son. I know that you can. I know you have the power to save him. Please! Give me that one request.' But he was silent."

My friend continues, "To this day I'm not sure why God didn't answer my request. I still wonder why. I'm not sure there is really a reason God could give me. What I do know is that God hurts with us. Our loss is his loss."

> I begged God, "Today I need you to save my son." But he was silent.

In their anger and hurt, Chris said there was a still, small voice inside him and his wife that said, "God gave you this child. It's his to take away."

I sat with Chris at the hospital that day. I watched as he shifted into autopilot to move through the next days and weeks. I wept for Chris and Kim and prayed with them. I saw how deep a crater Caden's death had left in their hearts.

Countless moments of grief came at them from nowhere. The sense of loss touched everything in their lives.

As the months passed, they began to work through the stages of grief. They had times of guilt, anger, rage, hurt, and just plain numbness. It was hard for them to understand what they were feeling and how to deal with it in a healthy way.

Kim had been feeling sick at one point and was convinced she had the flu, but her sister surprised her and said, "Kim, you don't have the flu. You're pregnant."

Kim dismissed the idea, saying, "Okay, you're a schoolteacher. I paid a lot of money to a man who specializes in this, and he said there is no way." But she decided to take a pregnancy test. She prepared herself emotionally for the test to be negative, as it had been countless times before. But this time, amazingly, it was positive. She couldn't believe it. Despite the fact that all the doctors had said it was impossible, she was expecting.

Later that year she gave birth to a beautiful little girl they named Claire. Chris said, "I kind of laughed the first time I held Claire. It was a laugh to say, 'God, I get it. You've called us to follow you. Not to make sense out of all the stuff going on. Not to understand it.' As I held Claire for the first time, I was blown away by the miracle of birth. It was God saying, 'I'm with you.'"

Now, it's not as though Claire was an even exchange

for Caden. It's not as though having Claire meant not griev-ing the loss of Caden. In a way, it actually intensified the loss they were still trying to make sense of. But in the gift of Claire, the Tretheweys learned that even though they did not know why things happened as they did, they had settled the *who* question. They knew they could trust God, and they derived their strength from him.

SOVEREIGN GOD

When our world falls apart and the pain of life settles in, yes, we are looking for explanations and meaning and ra-tionale, but even more so we want as-surance. Yes, we want answers. But these cries of pain, whether to God explicitly or just into the universe, are evidence of an implicit trust that something or someone greater— someone with answers!—is out there. Our hearts are rocked by regrets, sin, failures, and flaws, and in our distress we ache for resolution, restoration, and renewal.

> Cries of pain are evidence of an implicit trust that someone greater— someone with answers!—is out there.

A battle is waged within us with every *why* question we've entertained. *Why me? Why, God, didn't you* _____ *(fill in the blank)? Why was the person texting while driving? Why didn't the doctors catch it sooner? Why didn't the chemo work? Why did he leave me and the kids? Why?* But the danger with *why* questions is that they lead to a dark, confusing, frustrating, lonely, disconnected place.

Think about it. Does *why* bring healing? Does *why* bring closure? Rarely. *Why* keeps you in the past and blocks you from moving forward. *Why* keeps you stuck in the pain and chokes out the potential to heal. This is the reason that the better question—the question Christians should move into sooner rather than later—is *who*. Who is in charge? Who's in control? Who has all things in his hand? Who will make all things right? Who is restoring all things?

The Bible answers this question clearly and profoundly. One of the starkest, most beautiful pictures of God's sovereign rule comes from the apostle Paul in Colossians 1:15–18:

Christ is the visible image of the invisible God.
He existed before anything was created and
is supreme over all creation,
for through him God created everything
in the heavenly realms and on earth.
He made the things we can see
and the things we can't see—
such as thrones, kingdoms, rulers, and authorities
in the unseen world.
Everything was created through him and for him.

He existed before anything else,
    and he holds all creation together.
Christ is also the head of the church,
    which is his body.
He is the beginning,
    supreme over all who rise from the dead.
    So he is first in everything.

What a breathtaking piece of poetry this is! And what a bedrock of comfort it can be to know that Christ "existed before anything else, and he holds all creation together"! That's what we *really* want to know when life feels as if it's tearing apart. Is someone holding it together? Because we know *we* sure can't.

Although we pop out of our mommies believing the universe revolves around us, the entire time God is working in each person and each event and each second of every day to his own ends. Nothing happens beyond his watch; nothing takes him by surprise. God announces as much when he says,

Remember the things I have done in the past.
    For I alone am God!
    I am God, and there is none like me.
Only I can tell you the future
    before it even happens.

Everything I plan will come to pass,

    for I do whatever I wish.[2]

This means that, before time began, before God even created the world, he was aware of what every millisecond in the future would hold. And before any of us came to be, he knew who we were, what we would do, what we would think, and even how many hairs are on our heads at each fluctuation. (And believe me, the older I get, the more fluctuations there are!)

We find affirmation of God's control over the universe throughout the pages of Scripture, from the opening lines of his work of creation to the closing lines of his judgment and restoration. God upholds at every second the entire structure of the world. He established the earth on its foundation, bounded the sea, and created the light. He knows and rules the most obscure recesses of the earth, including the hidden depths, the distant horizons, the light and the darkness, and the heights. He oversees the blackest pools in the deepest caverns, where marvels of bioluminescence will never be seen by human eyes, and the thinnest-air peaks, where even birds do not perch. He manipulates Saturn and Venus and planets in solar systems we will never discover. He holds in his sovereign hand black holes and wormholes in outer space, juggles quarks and protons, pulls the levers of inner space and hyperspace. When a tree falls in the woods and nobody is around, *he* hears it. In short, God created all the elements of heaven and earth and steers them to his own ends.[3] Nothing happens away from God's watchful eye. Everything happens because God wills it or allows it, and nothing happens that God cannot either stop or redeem.

Not only is God in control, but God created the world for the purpose of displaying his worth, beauty, and glory. The ultimate mindfreak is not Criss Angel, although some of his magic is pretty freaky. The ultimate mind-freak is realizing that the universe is truly, utterly, and completely about God—and thus not about me—and then finding my greatest happiness in celebrating this reality. The Bible says, "Everything comes from [God] and exists by his power and is intended for his glory. All glory to him forever!"[4] It is not that some things or a few things are intended for his glory but that *everything* exists to give God glory.

> Nothing could be more important in this time of self-help and reality television and Facebook status updates and Twitter tweets and indie everything than realizing that we are not the main attraction of this world.

As we understand this, our framework shifts from being me-centered to being God-centered. The universe was not created for us but for him. Nothing could be more important in this time of self-help and reality television and Facebook status updates and Twitter tweets and indie everything than realizing that we are not the main attraction of this world. The world does not revolve around us, as much as we would like to think it does. Our daily challenges and decisions become opportunities to live for God's glory. As we reorient our lives around God, we have the opportunity more and more to join creation in turning up the volume on God's worth. This is the single most important lesson I've learned in my own valleys. By reorienting everything back to where it belongs—around God—I find my footing again.

So what about evil? Does God's rule mean that he created evil? Does it mean he authored it or orchestrates it?

The Bible is crystal-clear that God is holy and righteous; there is no slice of sin in his being at all, and there never will be. We can deny that God authored evil and affirm at the same time that he rules over it. To say that God can control, stop, use, or allow evil is not the same as saying that evil comes from him. While this tension of truth may be hard to maintain without more questions arising, we can find great assurance in knowing that, whatever comes to pass, even sin is accounted for by God. He will punish it or redeem it or both.

This means that the God you trust and love, the one

who is worthy and beautiful, can protect you. Though you may face all kinds of evil and pain in your life, you do not have to live in fear. No matter what happens—no matter what a terrorist does or which nations go to war or what befalls the country—you can rest in the arms of God. No darkness, no evil, no hate, no destruction, no calamity strikes without the permission of God. He is good. He does not do evil. He does not commit any crimes against you or his own holiness. He is in control. If you love God and delight in him and trust him, this is nothing but wonderful news.

If God were not in control, if he did not set the boundaries, you'd have reason to fear just about everything. As it is, though, the Bible challenges us to fear God, not people.[5] When the stock market crashes, when depression creeps in, when a horrible tragedy strikes, you are not alone. You can live in perfect peace today, knowing that no matter what happens tomorrow, it won't happen outside the range of God's watchful eye. He neither slumbers nor sleeps. He knows all things and providentially oversees all things.

> God isn't sitting in heaven wringing his hands in fear. He is bringing his plan to fruition.

This world is not spiraling out of God's control. It isn't barreling ahead into an unknown future with a powerless

God at the helm. God isn't sitting in heaven wringing his hands in fear. He is bringing his plan to fruition. He is working in our world each day to bring himself glory. In due time he will overthrow Satan, sin, and death.

LETTER TO GOD

Four years after Kim and Chris Trethewey faced the loss of Caden, they had an opportunity to spend a week at Blessing Ranch, a place for people to experience healing. You see, life had moved on, but Chris was still stuck.

Chris was not wrestling with the who. He got it. What he couldn't quite grasp was the why. *Why* haunted his every thought.

That week at the ranch saved his life, his marriage, his family, and the ministry God had called him to. During the week Chris was given three simple homework assignments. All three were letters that he was supposed to write. The first was a letter from him to his son. The second letter was by Chris and his wife from the point of view of what they thought Caden would say to them. The third letter? A letter from Chris to God. Chris shared with me that initially he thought the homework was pointless and verged on psychobabble. Yet the experience brought overwhelming healing.

Here is part of the letter that Chris wrote to God:

Heavenly Father,

I am not sure exactly where to start, what should be or needs to be said. I guess I ask that you will just guide my heart and my thoughts.

First, I know you are God. Your ways are perfect, flawless, without fault. I am totally confident in that. I know that you have the ability to take the circumstances that occur in life and use them for your good. I guess that is why I find myself pulled in opposite directions. I find myself totally relying on your will—which I know is perfect. I can grasp the thought that you have called the willing to step out in faith. But faith so many times just doesn't make sense. I know the stories in the Bible. Abraham and his son Isaac and that long walk up the mountain. Joseph being sold into slavery. You just call us to follow. To be willing. I get that.

But why Caden? No, I don't blame you for his death. I know that you didn't cause it. But why didn't you save him? Why didn't you work a miracle? Why didn't you reach out and touch him? Why didn't you flick that plug out of his airway so he could breathe? Why didn't you? I guess that is the question that can't be answered. But I wonder, if you gave me the answer, would it resolve the hurt

I feel inside? Would it bring closure? Would the "answer" bring understanding? Would knowing draw me closer to you? Would comprehending the answer take away the longing to hold Caden again? I think the answer is simply...no. Understanding the "why" would probably bring with it another list of questions, hurts, and misunderstandings. Plus, no answer would ever help me understand the loss of my son.

I guess I have resolved in myself that you are God; I am not. You love me so very much—you hurt when I hurt. You experience loss when I experience loss. You grieve when I grieve. You totally understand the pain of losing a son.

Okay, one request. Could you wrap your big arms around Caden for me every morning and give him a hug for me? Could you whisper in his ear that I love him? Could you tuck him in at night for me? If you can do that for me, I have a peace inside knowing that he is okay because he is with you.

Chris's letter is deeply moving because it describes both his faith and his struggle. When we are left without answers, God is all we have. Sometimes our hurt is with God himself. And while we may desire a cut-and-dried answer for our suffering, part of the healing is found, not so much in getting an answer, but in asking the questions and crying out to God.

WORSHIP IN THE PAIN

What we are talking about, essentially, is worship. Whatever we trust in is what we worship. Whatever we place our hope in is what we worship. When life falls apart, when things tear apart, many of us retreat inward and trust ourselves to make it through. We're resilient. We're strong. This is a knee-jerk reaction when pain hits—to protect ourselves, to insulate ourselves, to fight our way out with our power and sensibilities. But healing is found in worship.

When life gets torn, we don't have to sit passively by (that can lead to more depression and despair), nor do we need to beat our fists against everything (that leads to bitterness and abuse). We can turn ground zero into a sanctuary of worship to God. As Paul says, "We can rejoice… when we run into problems and trials, for we know that they help us develop endurance. And endurance develops strength of character, and character strengthens our confident hope of salvation."[6]

How do you rejoice? Are we talking about cranking up the Katrina and the Waves hit "Walking on Sunshine" and bouncing off the walls? Well, sure, if you can swing it. But we all know that when life reeks, you don't feel joyful, you don't feel like dancing. You don't even know the steps! And that's why you have to follow God's lead. When the only music blaring is grief, sickness, divorce, abuse, addiction, or any other painful numbers, don't sit passively, and don't boil over with rage. Trust God's promises. Trust him even in the darkest hour, and worship him. He is in the lead, holding out his hand for you to follow him. He may lead you through the valley of the shadow of death, but he won't leave you there.

Perhaps it's time for you to sit down and write a letter to God, as Chris did. Express your heart with absolute transparency. Write about the struggle and confusion. Maybe it's time to admit that bottling it all up isn't working. Be honest with God. He can take it. He's a big boy. Whatever you are feeling, it's okay. Anger. Shock. Denial. Bitterness. Tell him about it. God can handle your pain. And meanwhile, you'll be worshiping him, even if it doesn't feel like it.

> We can turn ground zero into a sanctuary of worship to God.

In your suffering you may not understand the why, but now you know the who, and that's what really matters. When your life is torn, God is ready and waiting. He is there for you.

Reframing Your Expectations

W riter Camerin Courtney faced a period of disillusionment when life did not match her expectations of God and faith. Having grown up in church, with Bible stories tidily presented with flannel graphs, she and her church friends began to expect that the Christian life would be pleasant and comfortable. She wrote, "And then we grew up.... Bad things happened, sometimes even when we prayed and read our Bibles and didn't kill anyone."[1]

Been there? Done that?

There is a dangerous teaching lurking in many churches, beginning with the teaching of children, and it's all the more menacing because it has none of the obvious bling or outrageous promises of the health-and-wealth stuff. But it does set up the Christian life as one in which obedience merits blessings. And while it is true that God blesses obedience, he often doesn't bless it in the way we have come to expect. Christians who do their best to love God and love their neighbors, who read their Bibles, who go to church, who give to charities, who volunteer in ministry, and who are routinely nice to everyone have terrible things happen to them. No one is immune to life's rawness. Yet this can be a difficult truth for those who have been led to believe otherwise.

One of the main beliefs that leads to this spiritual frustration is that God is close when things are great but far when things are bad. This portrays a God who is too clean to mess with messy people or too good to do good to bad people. Of course, God is perfectly clean and perfectly good, but the great news of Jesus is that this same God has chosen to get involved in the lives—and the messes—of everyday people. The great news is that God is in the pigsty with prodigal sons and daughters. He is the God of mess as much as he is the God of beauty, and, in fact, he is the God who makes the mess beautiful.

Camerin discovered this as she sought God in the details of life unexpected. How did she navigate through her unmet expectations? "I...listened to friends who'd been through crises.... Messy stories and untidy details, but peace and hope in the journey."

I'm a lot like Camerin in this regard. In my life there

have been many times when I expected God to do certain things for me, and when he didn't, I felt let down and disappointed. As I grew to recognize my false expectations and accept reality as it was, I rediscovered the power of a biblical view of God and faced my situation with reframed expectations and a renewed hope.

So that's the next step in trusting God when you hurt. After choosing to entrust our lives to a sovereign God even when we don't understand what's happening to us, the next step is to change how we think about the kind of life we're going to have on this earth. As a matter of fact, we have little choice.

> He is the God of mess as much as he is the God of beauty.

THE NEW NOW

Life is messy. There's no avoiding that. We're going to find ourselves in some dark, doubtful, or depressing places. This will challenge our expectations. But when we align them with the Bible, when we realize that God never promised us a house on Easy Street in this life, it is oddly comforting. We can accept this new now, this reality of loss or pain or difficulty. To live in denial is to avoid what God wants to do in us. In fact, the Bible tells us, "The more we suffer for Christ, the more God will shower us with his comfort through Christ."[2] We can expect difficulty, and we can find comfort in it.

When we are hurting, our minds may focus too much on how things were before. But if we spend too much time thinking about the peace before, we may prolong the process God is using to bring us to the next peace. If we focus too much on longing for the past, we may miss out on what God is doing now.

There are no time machines. What's past is past. There's no way to go back, to redo, to alter what was said or done. And some damage done in the past cannot be fixed. Maybe you are facing such damage right now. Maybe your marriage is broken and your ex has remarried or moved on in such a way as to never commit to you again. Maybe you've lost your dream and you realize there's no getting it back.

You can't do anything about what is already done. And you can't control others. So it makes little sense to keep spinning your wheels thinking you're going to end up in reverse. That now is over. There is a new now. All you can control is what you say and do in the present and what you expect of God.

GOD OF THE MESS

In the Bible when Job lost everything, he held on to his faith. Instead of bailing on God when all his expectations were dashed, he worshiped and made a remarkable declaration: "I came naked from my mother's womb, and I will be naked when I leave. The LORD gave me what I had, and the LORD has taken it away. Praise the name of the LORD!"[3]

I've reflected on this statement again and again, and I don't think I'll ever get to the bottom of it. This is a deep thought, way deeper than anything Jack Handey ever cooked up with his deep thoughts on *Saturday Night Live*. Job's statement reveals bravery, a deep view of God's sovereign rule, a liberating perspective of life in orbit around God. I find it incredibly humbling. The statement stands in stark contrast to our feel-good American faith. The God of the Bible isn't Aladdin, waiting for us to rub his lamp and make a wish. God is beautiful in his infinite wisdom, even when we are at a loss for why we're experiencing something.

Christians understood this better in previous generations. I was struck by this fact while reading Augustine's fifth-century classic the *City of God.* In the first part of the book, he describes Christians being killed, tortured, and raped during the fall of Rome and challenges those who argue that this proves the Christian God is powerless. Augustine systematically shows the foolishness of the argument, and as he does so, he speaks of a

> God is beautiful in his infinite wisdom, even when we are at a loss for why we're experiencing something.

Christian who does not "grieve if deprived in life of those possessions which he would soon have to leave behind at his death." Many were tortured to determine where they had hidden their gold or silver, but faithful Christians did not hope in money. They rejoiced in God even in their horrible situation.

Some of these believers starved to death, and others were destroyed by horrible diseases. Yet they remained steadfast in their allegiance to God. Strap in, and think about what Augustine wrote:

> Death is not to be regarded as a disaster, when it
> follows on a good life, for the only thing that makes
> death an evil is what comes after death. Those who
> must inevitably die ought not to worry overmuch
> about what accident will cause their death, but
> about their destination after dying. Christians
> know that the death of a poor religious man, licked
> by the tongues of dogs, is far better than the death
> of a godless rich man, dressed in purple and linen.
> Why then should those who have lived well be
> dismayed by the terrors of death in any form?[4]

To me this reads more like the script of William Wallace in *Braveheart* than the average believer's script for what it means to follow God. Christians in the Western world need to be challenged by this broader perspective of God and his work. Spending time in the *City of God*, I find myself asking forgiveness for clinging to the illusion of control in my life (and for getting so frustrated when Starbucks messes up my drink order). I pray for the strength and courage shown by those in previous times. They lived with a greater awareness of life's fragility and uncertainty that led to greater dependence on God and more radical faith. Suffering and even death were not things to fear but rather opportunities to bring glory to God.

This is not an incidental point but one that is integral to how we characterize the works of God. Sometimes in our *why* questions we imply that what God has done is unjust or unfair. In such cases, while our hurt and confusion are understandable, we must be careful not to apply our own sense of justice to God, as if he must match our expectations and desires. Because God is God, he may do as he pleases even if we don't understand it or agree with it.

> Because God is God, he may do as he pleases even if we don't understand it or agree with it.

The Bible tells us, "Whatever is good and perfect comes down to us from God our Father, who created all the lights in the heavens. He never changes or casts a shifting shadow."[5] The good stuff of life is from God—from love and friendship to guitars and even Apple products. This may not take away your pain and suffering in the least, but understanding this essential point is integral to the faith that will get you through your pain and suffering.

LOANERS

Another important expectation to reframe is that when God puts people, things, and experiences in our lives, he does not give them to us to own. I know it's weird to think of people or ministries or a sense of well-being as loaners, but that's what they are. An even better way to look at them might be as blessings God gives us the privilege to manage. In that sense, we are given and must take responsibility for people and things, but we do so only while recognizing that they still belong to God.

> When God puts people, things, and experiences in our lives, he does not give them to us to own.

One evening my dear friend Kurt and his seven-year-old son, Austin, made their way to the couch to allow their food to digest before they jumped into their nightly wrestling match. Without warning, Austin's robust seven-year-old frame went completely stiff, his eyes rolled back, and he became unresponsive. The ninety-second seizure crept by in a slow-motion, frame-by-frame episode of fear, confusion, and disbelief.

Kurt was confounded as he held his seizing son. But then, as quickly as the seizure had started, it stopped.

They had only a brief thirty seconds of reprieve before a second seizure hit with as little warning and with as much vigor as the first one. By the fourth seizure, panic had set in.

Kurt and Kelly jumped into the car with Austin and rushed to the hospital. Hour after hour the medical staff tried to get the seizures to stop.

The CT scans eventually came back with sobering results. The doctors had discovered two areas on Austin's brain that consisted of scar tissue created by two strokes he had while in the womb. Why, after seven years as a healthy boy, did Austin suddenly begin having seizures? Why did no one catch the problem while he was in the womb? Why didn't they catch it when he was born? These were just the beginning of a never-ending list of questions that had few answers.

Months raced by. The prescribed medication had little effect on the ever-increasing number of seizures that Austin was experiencing. At the peak he endured as many as one hundred seizures a day. Kurt was fully aware that at any moment one of these seizures could hit Austin's diaphragm, taking his life. That fear grew. Hopelessness crept in. Every search for answers seemed to lead to a dead end.

Dozens of appointments, scans, expert opinions, and medical diagnoses finally led to brain surgery as the only option. The surgeons were to perform a cortical resection of the right frontal lobe. In simple terms they needed to take out a half-dollar-sized piece of Austin's brain.

I, along with our entire church, prayed for Kurt and Kelly and Austin. We lifted thousands of prayers before God. We cried out to him to intervene and to heal.

The night before the surgery, Kurt left his wife and parents at the hospital and made his way to his hotel room. He had one thing on his mind. He and God had some deal making to do.

Kurt knew that making a deal with God is not good theology. He knew God probably looked down on it. But those who have gone through a moment in life this intense—filled with this depth of nauseating fear—can sympathize with Kurt's desire to do whatever it took.

This hurting father looked up with a terrified and broken spirit and prayed, "God, if my son can't come through this healed, alive, normal, take whatever you want from me. It might be selfish. I might sound like a martyr. I just don't know if I can handle him not being the same kid after this surgery as before. I can't live with myself knowing that I made the decision for the surgery to happen and I was responsible for messing up my son's life." All that night in a Chicago hotel room, Kurt and God wrestled.

Kurt was there when Austin woke up after surgery. He was thrilled to see that the boy had normal control of his body, his speech, and his mind. The doctors were extremely pleased and hopeful. The recovery time was thirty-five days. After that he could head home. For more than thirty days, he didn't have a single seizure. Not one.

Then the day before they were to head home, Austin had a seizure. No one was too worried. It was expected. And over the next year and a half, the seizures settled into a manageable one to two a week. This was dramatically better than the eighty to a hundred per day he had been suffering before the operation. Austin regained his lost weight. He went back to school. Life got back to normal.

Just when we all thought Austin was out of the woods, the seizures came back with a fury never experienced before. Months went by as the same processes and tests were completed again. Another brain surgery was scheduled as the only option to rescue Austin's life. This time the surgeons would take out even more of his brain.

The day of the operation came. Kurt went into the surgical area with his son and stayed as long as he could. He said good-bye and walked out of the operating room. Déjà vu hit. This was all happening again, yet with greater potential consequences. Just as Kurt was pulling off his scrubs, a nurse ran out of the swinging operating room doors. The man pulled down his mask and looked squarely in Kurt's eyes and said, "I'll take good care of your boy. Promise."

"Part of me had more faith in that dude than God," Kurt shares. "Why? Because why did God let this come back? Was this problem too big for God to handle? There was only one other option: God chose to not fix it."

I sat with Kurt and the family that day in the waiting room. Time crept by. We waited and whispered private prayers under our breath. Finally the doctor came out to say the surgery had gone well. There were no complications, and Austin's speech and motor skills were minimally affected. The bad news came over the following weeks when the seizures didn't stop. The seizures didn't even decrease in number. They actually increased. Plain and simple, the surgery hadn't worked.

Have you ever prayed and God was silent? Have you ever prayed and your prayers weren't answered? Have you kept praying the same prayer over and over with the same response? That is where Kurt, Kelly, and thousands of people—including me—are right now in praying for Austin. The prayers for complete healing haven't worked. There are no more options, no more surgeries, no more medications. Either a miracle happens and their son is healed, or the seizures will finally capture a life.

Kurt admits, "Do I get angry with God? Do I go places in my mind? Do I question God? Yeah. But have I ever let it go dark? Never! Because I love God. He saved my life. He gave me Austin in the first place. I have never felt that God has shoved my situation off his desk."

Kurt often lies back, cranks up some black gospel music, and closes his eyes and worships. The environment of brokenness and pain from which the songs come bring him comfort. The music resonates with his own feelings of needing God desperately.

"My wife and I still pray that God will heal Austin and make it better," Kurt says. "But Jesus knows what it is like to sit in the garden and beg for his life and hear God say no. So far God has said no. I don't like it, but I accept it."

Kurt understands that the sufferings of this world, serious as they are to us, are still just a vapor compared to the hope of heaven and God's plan for eternity. He believes that God understands his pain because his own Son suffered and died. God gets it. We are all torn up by what is happening, but together we are trusting God in the middle of it.

> The sufferings of this world, serious as they are to us, are still just a vapor compared to God's plan for eternity.

What do we call this perspective? This cry of the heart, this lament of pain, this desperately wanting everything back the way it was, even as eventually and in some cases simultaneously we say, "God, we belong to you"? I think it sounds a lot like accepting the new now and living like Jesus.

A LARGER PERSPECTIVE

Let's picture Jesus in the Garden of Gethsemane mere minutes from his arrest, mere hours from his crucifixion. As Jesus is anticipating the brutal agonies of the cross, we find him praying in pain but also in devotion to God's sovereignty. "'Abba, Father,' he cried out, 'everything is possible for you. Please take this cup of suffering away from me. Yet I want your will to be done, not mine.'"[6]

Jesus was asking the Father to take away the cup of pain. He was hoping for another option besides the cross, a way that would not bring such loss. In the end, however, he acknowledged that the Father owns time and what happens in it. And if it was the Father's will for salvation to come by the cross, Jesus was willing to submit to it. We see this attitude even on the cross itself, where Jesus said both, "My God, my God, why have you abandoned me?" and, "Father, I entrust my spirit into your hands!"[7]

> No matter how much suffering we face here on earth, because of the resurrection of Christ, our hope and final deliverance are secure.

We can find comfort in Christ in our moments of

deepest pain. He was not forced to suffer. Rather, he put himself in a position alongside us, identifying with us, to redeem us from our suffering. No matter how much suffering we face here on earth, because of the resurrection of Christ, our hope and final deliverance are secure. God has not promised paradise in this world but a redemption of it and paradise in the world to come.

REVISED EXPECTATIONS

For too long I viewed God like a genie I could make wishes to. I had false expectations of both God and the faith journey. I thought if I followed Jesus, I'd be happy and healthy and would face fewer big problems. As long as I was clean and sober, I reasoned, I could basically do what I wanted. My life would be all smiles, like the cover of a self-help book. But I also had doubts, questions, and fears, and I reasoned that if I just learned more of the Bible, these would disappear. I didn't realize that following God would mean learning to trust even as questions persist, that it would mean moving my family to Las Vegas of all places and often feeling like a missionary in another culture. I didn't grasp that there would be incredibly hard seasons, but I also didn't know that there could be so much joy in surrendering to God. Taking a hard look at my expectations and reframing them made a positive difference, because I realized more than ever that this world is not my home and I must not treat it as though it is. I'm just passing through.

Philip Yancey's book *Disappointment with God* states, "The Bible never belittles human disappointment..., but it does add one key word: temporary. What we feel now, we will not always feel. Our disappointment is itself a sign, an aching, a hunger for something better. And faith is, in the end, a kind of homesickness—for a home we have never visited but have never once stopped longing for."[8]

Take some time to consider your expectations of God and faith. You may realize that you need to adjust them, as I did. It's okay to face this and accept it.

Adjusting your expectations will help you acknowledge that there is a new now. Life may not look at all the way you pictured it. Nobody gets married thinking, *I'm going to divorce this person.* Nobody knows when a loved one will be taken away. But when those terrible moments come, it makes no sense to live in the past. That was reality then. This is the reality now. This is what God will use to begin rebuilding in you and around you.

> This world is not my home, and I must not treat it as though it is. I'm just passing through.

The good news, though, is that because God transcends all time, there is no moment outside his care and concern. Life for you may be ever changing, but our God is not. Your expectations may be shattered, but you can reframe them and discover hope, because not only is he the great I WAS and the great I WILL BE, but he also is the great I AM.

Life Interrupted

Scott Rigsby hit ground zero in a thunderous way, forcing him to figure out who was really in control of his life. He was eighteen years old and had just graduated from high school. Dreams and goals dominated his mind as his first semester of college was rushing closer. He was working for a landscaping company when tragedy struck. Scott was sitting in the back of a pickup truck, talking with his friends after a hard day's work, when the truck was hit by a passing eighteen-wheeler, throwing Scott underneath the attached three-ton trailer. After dragging him more than three hundred feet, the truck came to a stop.

The devastation to Scott's body was unthinkable. He had suffered third-degree burns on his back. His right leg was severed, and his left leg was severely mangled. And what happened to him emotionally turned out to be catastrophic.

Over the next twelve years, Scott had twenty-five surgeries and countless doctors' visits. Depression set in as he tried to manage a life filled with emotional and physical pain. Pain pills became his way to cope. He spent more than three years in a drug-induced haze.

During that period Scott had a conversation with a pastor friend. Later he didn't remember most of what they had talked about, but one thing stuck. Scott's friend had said to him, "God has a plan for your life." That simple statement led Scott to reconnect with God. He poured out his heart—everything he had ever felt and struggled with. Years of pain, questions, and anger that he had shoved deep inside erupted into a raw, unedited prayer. His extreme honesty allowed him to reconnect with God.

Scott's twenty-sixth surgery brought with it a turning point. It was the point when he decided not to be a professional patient but to get his life moving in a significant direction. You see, he had one good leg and one bad leg. His good leg was the leg he had lost in the accident. His bad leg was the one that had undergone countless surgeries. It was the leg that was causing him all the pain and problems. He made the bold decision to have the doctors remove that leg also. Talk about gutsy. Yet within six weeks he was not just walking but running on his new prosthetics. Scott's life had finally started a new chapter.

One day Scott prayed, "God, if you open a door for me,

I will run through it." A few days later Scott found himself in a bookstore, looking at the cover of a triathlete magazine. There was Sarah Reinertsen, a single-leg amputee who had just completed the Hawaii Ironman. Immediately Scott realized that God wanted him to do the unthinkable.

In seven weeks Scott finished six sprint-distance triathlons. From there he went on to become the first double amputee to complete an Olympic-distance triathlon. He also was the first double amputee to complete a full marathon. Those accomplishments in themselves were incredible, but Scott wasn't done yet. He set his sights on the ultimate challenge. He wanted to be an Ironman.

The full Ironman combines three disciplines at insane distances. Athletes have to complete a 2.4-mile swim, a 112-mile bike race, and a 26.2-mile run—all before the seventeen-hour time limit runs out. When the gun went off at the Ironman World Championship in Kona, Hawaii, Scott jumped in the water and began a journey that no double amputee had ever completed. Sixteen hours and forty-three minutes later, covering a total of 140.6 miles, and with only seventeen minutes until the cutoff time, Scott Rigsby crossed the finish line and became an Ironman.

> Scott found himself looking at the cover of a triathlete magazine. Immediately he realized that God wanted him to do the unthinkable.

"I had a dream that there were insurmountable odds," he said. "What I was trying to do was the unthinkable. But what I wanted to do was change the world. I wanted God to use my ordinary life. I wanted to place my ordinary life in the hands of an extraordinary God so that he could do extraordinary things."[1]

Scott learned to love God for who he is, not just for what he gives. He loved him for being righteous and true and strong. He loved him because he was worthy to be loved. He came to see that God was still at work in his pain and could be trusted.

So far we've seen the call to trust God and worship him even in our pain and struggles. We've considered our expectations and the need to reframe some of them. All of this is part of moving past being paralyzed with *why* questions and answering *who* with faith and trust. In this chapter let's put more skin on these themes by exploring the story of someone who, along with Scott Rigsby, knew what it meant to have life interrupted.

Job squared off with a new reality, and just when all hope seemed lost, God showed up to remind him that he'd been there all along.

The greatest biblical example of trusting God when torn is Job. He not only lost everything but also continued to worship in the midst of the pain. He expressed his doubts and feelings to God honestly.

Job's story tells us that pain is ancient. We will not be the first to go through it. We are not alone or abandoned in the trial, and our questions are as old as time. Job squared off with a new reality, and just when all hope seemed lost, God showed up to remind him that he'd been there all along. The Bible, for all its radical authenticity as well as its spiritual inspiration, contains much more power than self-help thoughts or positive thinking. That stuff is watermelon punch. The Bible is a syringe of adrenaline plunged straight into the heart.

THE GUY WHO HAD IT ALL

Job lived thousands of years ago. His story begins by telling us that "he was blameless—a man of complete integrity. He feared God and stayed away from evil."[2] Job was a good dude. He loved God, prayed for his family, and kept his word. He paid his bills on time, supported every school bake sale, and probably would have recycled if that had been an issue at the time. In fact, Ezekiel lists him with Noah and Daniel as one of the most righteous men of all time.[3]

On top of all this, he had plenty of bling, owning massive amounts of livestock, which shows he was a man with great status in the society of his day. "He was, in fact, the richest person in that entire area."[4] Job was loaded; he was the Warren Buffett of the ancient world, the Donald Trump of the Old Testament, minus the notorious comb-over.

Job had it all…but it was all about to change.

CRASHING THE PARTY

The story moves from Job living healthy and happy on earth to the heavenly realm. God was on his throne, and the angelic beings were assembling to file their reports. But there was a problem. An intruder named Satan crashed the party.

As you read through the Bible, you learn that Satan was an angel created by God. He turned on God because of pride in his heart and was consequently cast out of heaven. The Bible says that God will deal with Satan in the future. Hell was created for Satan and his angels.[5] A day of reckoning draws near. It is interesting that, in the original language, every time Satan's name appears, the definite article appears before it. So our translations could read "*the* Satan." The word *satan* means "accuser" or "adversary." The Satan, the Accuser, showed up and had a conversation with God.

God said, "Have you noticed my servant Job?"[6] It's as if God was bragging. "Have you seen Job? He's awesome! Job loves me. He is devoted to me, and there is no one like him."

Satan replied, "Yes, but Job has good reason to fear God. You have always put a wall of protection around him and his home and his property. You have made him prosper in everything he does. Look how rich he is!" Then Satan threw down: "But reach out and take away everything he has, and he will surely curse you to your face!"[7]

The implication is that Job loved God because of what God had given him. If those blessings were taken away, there would be nothing left. So God allowed Satan to test Job, with one limitation: "Do whatever you want with everything he possesses, but don't harm him physically."[8]

As Satan stood before God and pointed his finger at Job, his charge went right to the core of God's identity. If Job got roughed up, Satan reasoned, then he would publicly repudiate God.

After God set the boundary of physical protection, "Satan left the LORD's presence," implying that he left the Lord's presence immediately and went to work.[9] Later God would also allow Satan to affect Job physically.

> If God and Satan were in a boxing ring, God would resemble Muhammad Ali in boxing skill, and Satan would resemble SpongeBob SquarePants.

This interchange in heaven should remind us that God and Satan are not equal foes, squared off in a match that's anybody's game, dependent on how hard we pray or how good we can be. If God and Satan were in a boxing ring, God would resemble Muhammad Ali in boxing strength, agility, and skill, and Satan would resemble SpongeBob SquarePants. The comparison is laughable. It would be as ridiculous as Spider-Man going toe to toe with Barney or Wolverine fighting every character from *Yo Gabba Gabba!*—at once. (If you have a preschool kid, your stomach is nauseous just thinking about *Yo Gabba Gabba!*) There is no comparison between the two. God is in control. He is all-powerful. God owns Satan the way you or I might own a hamster.

Satan is the cause of much hurt and pain in our world, but he is not a rogue angel outside the control of God. This is a wonderful truth that brings me great hope. No tragedy, no temptation, no spiritual battle will cross my door without the prior knowledge and permission of God. As Martin Luther is believed to have said, "Even the devil is the Lord's devil."

This is just one of the insights about suffering that the story of Job gives us. There are many more.

CRUSHED

Suddenly the story of Job moves back to earth. A messenger came to Job and gave him word that robbers had stolen his oxen and donkeys, and not only that, but also they'd killed his servants. This would have been a staggering loss financially, of course, but also relationally, as these were Job's valued employees. Before Job had time to start assembling weapons and going all A-Team on the perpetrators, a second messenger arrived to say that lightning had come down and burned up Job's sheep and the shepherds. Job's herd of animals had gone from large to nonexistent. Before that messenger finished relaying this bad news, another messenger made Job aware that all his camels had been stolen and his camel herders killed.

Then came the worst news of all. The crushing blow. A fourth messenger came to make Job aware that his sons and daughters had been killed in the collapse of their house. All ten of them—gone.

Can you imagine such pain? Job was at the absolute ground zero of his life. Some of the shock at reading Job's story may be mitigated for us because we've already read of the encounter between God and Satan in the opening of the book. But Job didn't know anything about that. He didn't know about the spiritual realities behind the scenes in his story. For him, it was not a story anyway—it was his life! He was just going about his own business, and in one day the world unraveled. Sound familiar?

> Job was just going about his own business, and in one day the world unraveled. Sound familiar?

The first thing Job did when he hit ground zero was to take his pain to God. The Bible says he "stood up and tore his robe in grief."[10] Then he shaved his head. Hair was a picture of glory in the ancient world. (Remember, he didn't have Donald Trump's comb-over.) To shave one's head was to say, "My glory has gone. Everything I loved and worked for is gone."

Job knew exactly where to go in the crisis. He "fell to the ground to worship."[11] This was Job's moment of absolute calamity. He'd been preparing for this moment his entire life, and he didn't even know it. When the moment came, he thought, *I know only one place to go. There is only one source of power and strength and hope that I will turn to.* So he fell on his face, stretched out his hands, and worshiped God.

OUT OF THE WHIRLWIND

Throughout the story of Job, there are sections of intense questioning and struggling with the problem of evil and suffering. At the end of the book, Job was hanging out with his friends while a storm was rolling in. He'd been wailing and debating his unhelpful friends and waiting desperately on God. As this storm came upon them suddenly, "the LORD answered Job from the whirlwind."[12] God came to Job personally and responded.

One of the most remarkable things in the book of Job is that God showed up to speak at all. But when he did, his very presence communicated, "I've been with you all along. I know what you've gone through. I've heard everything you've said." This in and of itself proves that Job's friends' understanding of God was flawed. They had suggested that God would not hear Job because of his unrighteousness, and they had suggested that if God were to address Job, it would be in crushing judgment. Yet God did answer Job, and he answered him, not in judgment, but in a dramatic reversal of expectations that provided an exhilarating twist in Job's story.

The Lord spoke strongly to Job. For more than thirty chapters, Job and his friends had dialogued. Job had hurled questions at God. He'd said some things to God that were bold, presumptuous even. And when it was time for God to answer, he did so in a way that made Job's philosophical and emotional posturing seem downright puny.

God opened with a powerful question: "Who is this that questions my wisdom with such ignorant words?"[13]

I imagine Job was thinking, *Uh-oh, this does not look good.*

God continued: "Brace yourself like a man, because I have some questions for you, and you must answer them."[14]

"Brace yourself like a man." What the heck does that mean? Here was Job, who'd been ranting and venting and verbally vomiting all over everybody (because he was hurting), standing before God with festering boils and fearful longing, and God was basically telling him to put on a helmet. It was about to get heavy.

How heavy was it going to get? God would deliver two speeches to Job, asking him seventy-seven questions. And Job wouldn't be able to answer a single one of them. God fired off questions about creation, nature, space, and the universe. Things like "Can you direct the movement of the stars—binding the cluster of the Pleiades or loosening the cords of Orion?"[15]

Think about it. On any given night, you can see about thirty stars from downtown New York City, about three thousand from most rural areas, and up to thirty billion with a large telescope. We do not know how many stars exist, but we know there are over two hundred billion stars in our galaxy alone. One of the largest known stars has a diameter of almost a billion miles!

An explosion of energy on the surface of the sun, known as a solar flare, recently sent a magnetic cloud toward the earth at a million miles per hour. The cloud was over thirty million miles in diameter. Think of the size and speed of this cloud, and remember that God is bigger and faster. Best-selling author and researcher Dr. Richard Swenson wrote, "If we witness a magnetic cloud thirty million miles in diameter moving a million miles per hour—is

God bigger than that? Can He move faster than that? If the center of the sun has temperatures of fifteen million degrees centigrade and pressures of seven trillion pounds per square inch—could God walk into the core of the sun, take a nap, and walk back out? Every impressive structure or event in the universe should remind us of a God who is greater than all His works."[16]

The point God is making to Job is not simply that his creation is amazing but that he is so superior to his creation and faithfully oversees it. He's saying, remember who you are talking to! Maybe if we regularly spent time staring up at the vast expanse of the night sky and meditating on the God who established and upholds it, we would spend less time questioning his ability to comfort and console us. Maybe if we gave the Author and Artist of the universe the glory due him, we would not assail him with accusations when things get out of whack in our personal spheres of life.

> Maybe if we gave the Author and Artist of the universe the glory due him, we would not assail him with accusations when things get out of whack in our personal lives.

What's interesting is that, in all his questions to Job, God never really acknowledged the specific meaning behind the things Job had been through. He didn't say, "Job, let me explain to you that Satan came to me, and there was this whole conversation about the basis of your trust in me, and, well, to make a long story short, Satan was allowed to test you." He never answered the question of why people suffer and struggle. What God *did* do, fortunately for Job, was uphold his questions. God confirmed that Job had been directing his deepest questions to the strongest source. He affirmed Job's belief, acknowledging that he was both good and all-powerful.

Where was God when Job stood at the graves of his ten children and felt alone in the universe? Where was God when he grieved and he wailed and he mourned and he cried out and he heard nothing but silence in return? Where was God when he felt distant from God and distraught because of it?

We have the same kinds of questions.

Where is God while a friend grieves the loss of his dear wife of sixty-three years?

Where is he as a soldier in Afghanistan charges a hill he's been commanded to take while enemy fire whizzes all around him, claiming the lives of his friends? He wonders if he will ever make it back home to his kids.

Where is God when you go through seasons in your spiritual journey in which you just don't feel up to the task? You show up, go to church, and read your Bible. You jump through all the religious hoops, but you don't feel as if you're getting anywhere. Where is God in the midst of *that*?

The truth is that God was there for Job. And he is there for us too, closer than we realize.

GENEROUS GOD

Job's friends saw God as a curmudgeon, a miser, a traffic cop with a radar gun and a ticket quota. They misrepresented God, who is actually rich in mercy, grace, joy, and every other good and perfect gift. He is a big, big spender.

God restored to Job "twice as much as before." Twice as much! Before, he was the wealthiest guy in the area. Then he went from just bling to

> God is a big, big spender.

bling-bling. "The LORD blessed Job in the second half of his life even more than in the beginning. For now he had 14,000 sheep, 6,000 camels, 1,000 teams of oxen, and 1,000 female donkeys. He also gave Job seven more sons and three more daughters."[17] These blessings could never make up for the loss. One child can't simply be replaced by another. But they testify to God's grace and generosity in the midst of a horrible trial.

Read a little further: "Job lived 140 years after that, living to see four generations of his children and grandchildren. Then he died, an old man who had lived a long, full life."[18] Another way to put that might be, "He died an old man satisfied." God brought it all back full circle and then some. Job did not die a bitter, broken man. He died as someone filled with joy, trusting a God who saw him through every trial.

THE GOD WHO MENDS

We could read Job as a cautionary tale, teaching that trusting God does not mean an easy life—terrible things can still happen to us. But Job is more than that. It is the biography of a man who was broken and a biographical snippet of a God who fixes. The book of Job communicates the deep truth of pain and suffering but also the deeper truth of the God who transcends the fallen world, who was there before sin and brokenness entered the world and who will still be there when sin and brokenness are no more. And the book communicates the deep grace of God to bring us to that future time of endless joy alongside himself.

> Our loving God will fix what's broken, heal what's wounded, rebuild what's destroyed, cure what's diseased, mend what's torn, and raise what's dead.

We could read the end of Job in a karmic way ("Put good in, you'll get good back—eventually") or a sentimental way ("Just let go and let God") or a religious way ("If you push the right behavioral buttons, you'll get the desired blessings"). But God wants us to read it in a devotional way. No, I don't mean in a quiet time at five in the morning through morning breath and eye boogers (although that probably wouldn't hurt). What I mean is, because this is Scripture, God's revealed Word to us, we should read Job and see ourselves and God more fully, more authentically. This means seeing ourselves more desperately and seeing God more hopefully. Because we will be torn. And only God can mend us. And if we trust him "though he slay" us, he *will* mend us.[19]

What Job tells us is that our loving God will fix what's broken, heal what's wounded, rebuild what's destroyed, cure what's diseased, mend what's torn, and raise what's dead. We can risk trusting him even when things don't make sense. And when we do, we are acting in accord with what the Bible teaches. Trusting God when torn is the normative experience of believers throughout the Bible. It's okay if you can't figure out why; just keep hanging on to the God who is hanging on to you.

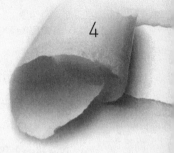

Courageous Trust

Brennan Manning, in his book *Ruthless Trust,* shares a story about one of the most brilliant students he ever taught: August Gordon. August has chosen a life that few people have even considered. He takes six months out of the year to live in seclusion in the Smoky Mountains. The other six months of his year he preaches for a mission outreach that is focused on feeding the hungry and homeless in Haiti, Jamaica, and other Caribbean islands.

On one of Manning's visits with August, Manning asked him a pointed question: "Gus, could you define the Christian life in a single phrase?" Think about that for a moment. What would you say? How would you answer that?

Without pausing August said, "I can define it in a single word: trust."

Manning goes on to expand on the concept of trust.

Unwavering trust is a rare and precious thing
because it often demands a degree of courage that
borders on the heroic. When the shadow of Jesus'
cross falls across our lives in the form of failure,
rejection, abandonment, betrayal, unemployment,
loneliness, depression, the loss of a loved one; when
we are deaf to everything but the shriek of our own
pain; when the world around us suddenly seems a
hostile, menacing place—at those times we may
cry out in anguish, "How could a loving God
permit this to happen?" At such moments the seeds
of distrust are sown. It requires heroic courage to
trust in the love of God no matter what happens
to us.[1]

The security we have in our darkest times comes not
only from knowing that God is in control but also from
knowing that God loves us. What good would it do us to
have a sovereign God who was ambivalent or wishy-washy?
We can hope and trust—we can rebuild from a broken
home, a broken dream, a broken marriage, or a broken
heart—not just because God is God but also because God
is good.

The God Who Is Love

First John 4:8 tells us that "God is love." He doesn't just have love or give love; he *is* love. Elsewhere in God's Word we learn that Jesus "is our peace."[2] We will find all the best attributes and virtues life has to offer in the Giver of Life. *He* is the way; *he* is the truth; *he* is the life.

Trusting these characteristics of God can make a world of difference when life just flat-out stinks. Because when we're hurting, it's not just the hurt that hurts but also the sinking feeling we sometimes have that God doesn't care, that he has gone AWOL, or—worse—that he is actively out to get us. When we are suffering or struggling, Satan will tempt us to think that God is powerless or loveless. He wants us to use our pain as evidence against God. Instead, our pain should drive us into God, because nobody heals like God, and nobody loves like God.

> Our pain should drive us into God, because nobody heals like God, and nobody loves like God.

Take a look at some of the following promises from the Bible. They are just a sampling of the good stuff about our good God.

- "The LORD is close to the brokenhearted; he rescues those whose spirits are crushed."

- " 'I know the plans I have for you,' says the
  LORD. 'They are plans for good and not for
  disaster, to give you a future and a hope.' "
- "Anyone who harms you harms my most
  precious possession."
- "Give all your worries and cares to God, for
  he cares about you."
- "The love of the LORD remains forever with
  those who fear him."
- "The faithful love of the LORD never ends! His
  mercies never cease."[3]

That last verse comes from the book in the Bible called
Lamentations, a book named for mourning, full of heart-
felt cries of pain, anxiety, and desperation. Yet it contains
the proclamation that even when troubles come, God's love
is still there and still rock steady. His love for us does not
waver as our love for him does. His concern for us does not
shift like the sands of time. His grace for us does not rise
and fall like our emotions. He is always there, and he always cares.

TRUST IN THE MIDST OF ILLNESS

Tony Snow, a cable news anchor and press secretary for President George W. Bush, was diagnosed with colon cancer.
He shared about moving past the *why* questions in faith.

We shouldn't spend too much time trying to answer the why questions: *Why me? Why must people suffer? Why can't someone else get sick?* We can't answer such things, and the questions themselves often are designed more to express our anguish than to solicit an answer.

I don't know why I have cancer, and I don't much care. It is what it is—a plain and indisputable fact.... Our maladies define a central feature of our existence: We are fallen. We are imperfect. Our bodies give out.

But despite this—because of it—God offers the possibility of salvation and grace. We don't know how the narrative of our lives will end, but we get to choose how to use the interval between now and the moment we meet our Creator face-to-face.[4]

Though we all desire a trouble-free life, Snow reminds us that "God likes to go off-road." God most often comes near to his children and ministers to their needs when they're in the wilderness. It was true in biblical times, and it's true today. And when rich, famous, happy Tony Snow found himself in the wilderness, he wasn't trusting science, despite availing himself of its advances, and he wasn't trusting friends, despite staying close with them and valuing their company. He was trusting God. But not just any ol' god. He was trusting the one true God, the God who preserves us by his love.

Jesus said to his disciples, "What is the price of two sparrows—one copper coin? But not a single sparrow can fall to the ground without your Father knowing it. And the very hairs on your head are all numbered. So don't be afraid; you are more valuable to God than a whole flock of sparrows."[5] In this passage we hear Jesus confirming the sovereignty of the Father. He is all-seeing and all-knowing, vast enough to control the universe but specific enough to know how many hairs are on our heads. But we also hear Jesus confirming the love of the Father. We are *valuable* to him.

On another occasion Jesus explained to his followers, "I have told you all this so that you may have peace in me. Here on earth you will have many trials and sorrows. But take heart, because I have overcome the world."[6] Again we see the affirmation of sovereignty—Jesus will overcome the world—coupled with the promise of peace and the encouragement to "take heart." Why? Because God doesn't just control the world; he loves it.

> When the world is crumbling around us, what sustains us is the deep, deep love of God.

The world keeps turning, but God's love stays strong. Our hearts get swept away, but God's heart remains for the broken and the weary. Our love is unpredictable, but God's love is steadfast. It never stops. His love will chase us to our dying day and will pursue us into the heavenly life that comes after death.

When the world is crumbling around us, what sustains us is the deep, deep love of God. In his book *How Long, O Lord?* D. A. Carson wrote,

> Consider Paul: he prays three times that his "thorn in the flesh" (whatever that is) will be taken away. When I was a child, I was told that God normally had three answers: yes, no, and wait. It seems safe enough: God can't lose, no matter what happens. But that is not God's answer to Paul. God's answer was this: "My grace is sufficient for you, for my power is made perfect in weakness" (2 Cor. 12:9).
>
> Eventually Paul does not merely put up with this answer: he exults in it. His heart's cry is that in his own life and ministry he might experience the same power that raised Jesus from the dead (Phil. 3:10). Here he learns the secret of it: God's power is made perfect in Paul's life when Paul himself is weak.[7]

This is no arbitrary work of power. God is ultimately concerned for his own glory, yes, but he has determined that his glory will be made manifest in our restoration. It is God's *gracious* power that is sufficient for us. It is his power *in our lives* that gives us cause to fight for joy.

Nevertheless, there will come a day when those who trust in Jesus for salvation will have all their weaknesses erased, all their tears wiped away, all their fears eliminated, and all their pain and brokenness healed. This, too, shall pass. But "love will last forever!"[8]

TRUE LOVE

In the cult classic *The Princess Bride,* there is a great scene between Inigo Montoya and Miracle Max. Westley is almost dead, yet Montoya needs him to live so that he can help avenge his father. Miracle Max, played by Billy Crystal, won't help unless he is paid enough money or has a good enough cause.

After pumping air into Westley's mouth, Miracle Max bends over and asks, "Hey. Hello in there. Hey, what's so important? What ya got here that's worth living for?" Miracle Max then gently pushes on Westley's chest.

Two words slowly leak from Westley's mouth. "Truuue looovvve."

Montoya excitedly says, "True love. You heard him. You could not ask for a more noble cause than that."

Miracle Max comes back and says, "True love is the

greatest thing in the world. Except for a nice MLT—mutton, lettuce, and tomato sandwich—when the mutton is nice and lean and the tomato is ripe." (What a great movie!)[9]

True love *is* the greatest thing in the world, but this is not the love that you and I manipulate and pervert for our own selfish satisfaction. It is the true love that God embodied before the world was created. It is a love that is selfless. It is a love that does not have conditions or expectations. It is a love that is pure and holy. It is a love that does not go inward but is always focused on others. It is a love that gave everything for you, for me. It is a love that reflects the essence of who God is.

We often have a messed-up picture of God, like a cosmic version of Spock in *Star Trek*, ruthlessly rational and coldly logical about anything emotional. Sometimes we believe he's standoffish, disconnected. Do you see a bland, stoic God with no ability or inclination to sympathize with your weaknesses? Well, cut it out! That's not God. That's not how he responds to people in the Bible.

> Do you see a bland, stoic God with no inclination to sympathize with your weaknesses? Well, cut it out!

I love the story of Lazarus. Jesus and Lazarus were buddies. Jesus arrived in Bethany after Lazarus had died following a lengthy illness. There, Jesus met the family and friends at Lazarus's tomb. He was grieved deeply. One of the most powerful verses in the Bible is one of the shortest verses: "Then Jesus wept."[10]

This verse gives me hope, because deep down I don't really want a God and Savior who is going to just pat my head and offer a trite, "It's going to be okay." I want a God who understands my pain. I want a God who is honest about the fact that we are going to have trouble in this world.[11] I want a God who is going to embrace my emotions and feel them alongside me.

Jesus didn't dismiss his friends' pain. He didn't try to explain it away or minimize it. He entered into it fully, experiencing it himself. He wept. Then he raised Lazarus from the dead.

He not only weeps with us, but he promises to one day raise us from the dead as well!

THE LIVING DEAD

In his deepest pain and deadly desperation, Job asked the most important question any of us could ask in such circumstances: "Can the dead live again?" He already felt dead inside, and due to his illness, he may have been thinking of the physical death that awaited. He was losing hope in success and prosperity and health and even family. He was clinging to the hope of all hopes: eternal life. *If I were to die,* he thought, *will I live again? Is there a life beyond this one, a better life?* And this is what he said about his hoped-for an-swer: "If so, this would give me hope through all my years of struggle, and I would eagerly await the release of death."[12]

If Job could only believe that the trouble in this world was not the end of all life, he would be immeasurably helped even in his trouble. He could have hope. If eternal life is true, it is cause to "rejoice with a glorious, inexpress-ible joy," even if this life is cause to lament with a grievous, inexpressible pain.[13]

But just as we will have trouble in this world, so we will also have glorious, inexpressible joy in the world to come. Yes, God wants Job (and us) to know that a person *can* live again. And, yes, this is cause for hope through all our years of struggle.

We can take great comfort in knowing that the God who is the ruler over our suffering is the same God who is the ruler over the redemption of all creation, who rules over joy as well as pain, blessings as well as curses, restoration as well as brokenness. The sovereign God of the cross is the sovereign God of the resurrection. And it is the resurrection that Job most looked forward to when he said this:

> As for me, I know that my Redeemer lives,
>   and he will stand upon the earth at last.
> And after my body has decayed,
>   yet in my body I will see God!

I will see him for myself.

Yes, I will see him with my own eyes.

I am overwhelmed at the thought![14]

This is what Job was saying: "Even if I may be dying, I know that my Redeemer lives. I know that my God is a defeater of death, and because of this, even if this body gets eaten up by worms and maggots, I'm gonna get a new one, an indestructible one. And I won't have to wonder about the distance of God, because my very own eyes will be able to look into his." (Yes, he really was saying all that.) And then he tacked this on to the end: "Whoa!"

When was the last time we were swept away by this thought?

We have even more clarity on the matter because of the testimony of the life, death, and resurrection of Jesus. We anticipate the victory of God in Christ. To be "in Christ" means that, not only do we share Christ's suffering, but also Christ shares ours in an important way: as Christ overcame, so will we.

The resurrection provides vindication for the suffering experienced by Christ on the cross. It is a concrete illustration—and an ultimate one—showing that God will win the victory. After Jesus uttered his cry of pain and was placed in the cold, dark tomb, his followers likely experienced something similar to what Job experienced. The one they had looked to as their deliverer and hope was suddenly pinned to that cruel Roman implement of death. Their desires and hopes were shattered. But God won the victory on the third day as Jesus Christ rose again.

The resurrection guarantees the deliverance of those who are suffering. If there were no resurrection, faith would be useless, and Jesus would be just another carcass. Yet in his resurrection, Jesus swallowed up sin and death with a conquest of eternal achievement and glory. Now our pain and suffering are put on notice because their days are numbered. The resurrection seals the victory of God and provides hope to those struggling with grief. As Martin Luther King Jr. once put it, "Christianity has always insisted that the cross we bear precedes the crown we wear." Jesus reminds us that all who mourn, who are meek, persecuted, hungry for righteousness—those are the ones who will be comforted.[15]

> God is able and eager to open up the new world of a pain-free, disease-free, trouble-free life on the other side of this one.

Though there is darkness in suffering, as when Jesus was lying in the tomb, a light will shine forth when God remembers his people, just as when Christ rose from the dead. The good news of God's control over suffering is that he is able and eager to open up the new world of a pain-free, disease-free, trouble-free life on the other side of this one. Knowing that truth and trusting in the Author of it are cause for great hope during all your days of struggle.

C. S. Lewis said that our longings for something more show that there are things that can satisfy those longings.[16] So while we may feel that our desire for all the things in the world to be "put to rights" is merely a utopian view of reality, the Bible testifies that our longings will be fulfilled in "the summing up of all things in Christ."[17]

God has a plan that he will accomplish. How will he, who did not spare his own Son but instead gave him up for our sins, not also give us graciously all good things? If it was the will of God to crush Christ on the cross and achieve victory for all who trust in Jesus, why should we fear that God will not seek our greatest good, even in suffering?

The Great Exchange

For those who are torn, perhaps the two greatest points of assurance we can have are that *God is there* and that *he loves us*. In the void of creation, he was there; at the void of the cross, he was there; in the void of our suffering, he is there. Not only is he there, but also he loves us deeply. Our pain will one day be washed away by the overwhelming tide of the victory of God in Christ.

At one point Job cried out in frustration, "I need someone to mediate between God and me, as a person mediates between friends."[18]

He had one. And so do we.

Jesus came as the mediator between God and us. He lived the perfect life that we couldn't live. He died a sacrificial death for us on a cross, paying a price for us so that we could be bought back from sin and death.

The truth our loving God reveals is this: we can be forgiven for our sins and be given a new start for our lives. Jesus reconciles us to close relationship with God. The Bible says that when you place your trust in Jesus's finished work on your behalf, you acknowledge that you are a sinner. You acknowledge that you are not perfect, that you have failed. You trust that Jesus lived and died and rose again *for you*.

> You can answer the question "Can the dead live again?" with an emphatic "Yes, and by faith *I will.*"

The Bible promises that in that act of faith a great exchange happens in which the righteousness of Christ is transferred to your account. You *can* live again, anew. Trusting Christ doesn't mean all your problems go away. But it does mean that Christ holds you in your problems, that he comes near to you in your suffering, that you can answer the question, "Can the dead live again?" with an emphatic, "Yes, and by faith *I will.*" That is heroic trust in the face of whatever life throws our way. That is going all the way in answering the *who* question in our lives.

AFTER *WHO?*

So far we've looked at key parts of trusting God when we're torn. We started with the importance of worship in our trials and surrendering our pain and our questions to God. Accepting where we are, we took a hard look at our expectations of God and our disappointments. Job illustrated many of these principles for us and took them further, reminding us that God is not finished with us and forcing us to acknowledge that God is so much bigger than our problems. He rules, and we're living in his world. But all this talk of God's rule and control needs to be informed by his love and goodness. So in this chapter we've considered the importance of trust by looking at more of why God is worthy of our trust. We trust him as one who rules, but equally essential, we trust him as one who is good, one who loves.

In the chapters to come, we'll turn our attention from whom we trust and why we trust him to how we can face our challenges and move forward. We'll consider some practical ways we can move forward and find healing, because God is both all-powerful and all-loving.

The first practical topic concerns living in community.

The fact is, there is no easy answer for dealing with our struggles and pain, but there is a wrong one—to do it alone. Trusting God is critical, as we have seen, but so is trusting others. In chapter 5 we'll learn that as we live in faith toward God, he challenges us to live with enough faith in others to share our struggles.

Part 2

Putting the Pieces Back Together

Share the Struggle

We live in a world that is processed, synthesized, faux, injected, artificial, dyed, enhanced, touched up, rumored, twisted, tainted, and edited. The lines between what is real and what is fake have been blurred beyond recognition.

Take something as essential to human existence as Easy Cheese. Easy Cheese is a substance resembling cheese that comes in a can. When added to Ritz Crackers, it is an eating utopia. On the outside of the can there is a label that states, "Made with Cheese." But is Easy Cheese a real cheese? Or is it an impostor of cheesealisciousness?

To resolve this quandary, you simply have to look at what the product is made of. Easy Cheese has a whopping seventeen ingredients, including things I've never heard of, such as annatto. Somewhere along the way, Easy Cheese stopped being cheese and became a processed, synthesized, chemically evolved substance that sends me into mouth-watering cravings. And, hey, it's "Made with Cheese," sort of.

Easy Cheese is not the only impostor. Shell out a mere two hundred dollars, and you can get yourself a bachelor's degree without taking one class. If you want a tan, you don't need the sun anymore. You want different-colored eyes? Tinted contacts will do the trick. Celebrity photos have been so touched up, Photoshopped, and enhanced that a picture doesn't always resemble the real person.

There is so much pressure on us to be fake. We are uncomfortable with pain and weakness, and therefore many of us feel that we have to compensate with some sort of stoic facade. We do our best to appear that all is well. We put Band-Aids on our pain. We employ simple solutions, apply a bumper-sticker theology that says, "Try Jesus, and it will make it all easy." We try to pretty up the mess of our lives and feelings, like sweeping dirt under a rug. But the dirt's still there.

> There is so much pressure on us to be fake. What we need is honest community with others.

Our approach to covering up our pain can actually feed behavioral extremes, as we lash out with dangerous behavior. We try to soothe our pain with sex or food or drugs or alcohol, or we try to medicate pain with achievement. We shoot for success in business or the large bank account or the big man or woman on campus status so that everyone will pay attention to those diversions rather than the hurting person behind the curtain. What we need, though, is honest community with others.

Me Too

Writer Anne Lamott said, "I think the message of Jesus is 'Me too.'" When we are struggling, hurting, wounded, limping, doubting, questioning, barely hanging on, moments away from crashing, Jesus can look us in the eyes and honestly say, "Me too. I've been there." And this can be transformative and healing for us. We can also turn to each other with, "Me too. I've struggled, and we're in this together."

My friend Tony is a pastor who works hard to create a church culture where people don't walk alone. Recently a special thing happened that demonstrates this principle.

Twenty-year-old Nicole is part of the church family and has leukemia. She had it as a teenager, and it went into remission, but it's back. Nicole is a beautiful girl who was going to enter the Miss California beauty pageant before she got the diagnosis. Now she is going through chemo, and her hair is falling out.

At a recent church gathering, the community let her know that she is not alone. They created a sixty-foot-long banner that everybody signed to wish her well. They told her how much they loved her. Then they bought her a computer, because she didn't have one and they wanted her to be able to stay connected with others in the church while she was in the hospital. They also raised some money to help pay her hospital bills. And several people in the church family shaved their heads! They cut off all their hair—men and women alike—to demonstrate solidarity with Nicole.

Wouldn't it have been tragic if Nicole had never shared about her leukemia returning? What if she had decided to suffer alone?

As believers in Jesus, we are to mourn with those who mourn, bear one another's burdens, and hurt when others hurt, and when we receive comfort, we are to pass it on.[1] It is meaningful and powerful when the church joins together to share in someone's pain and suffering.

No one should ever have to suffer alone. Take your pain and frustration honestly to God and to a few close friends. Don't sugarcoat it or beat around the bush; just lay it out there. That honesty is so important in acknowledging where you are and in finding a path to healing.

I struggle with sharing my doubts and fears with others, as most of us do. I stuff things and focus on the positive, often to my detriment. But sharing with close friends brings clarity and insight. I have also spent time with a Christian counselor and have found this to be important for me. It is not possible to process what we are experiencing and thinking in a healthy way without such honesty.

James 5:16 tells us, "Confess your sins to each other and pray for each other so that you may be healed." How is there healing in confessing to each other? Isn't confessing our sins to each other weird? embarrassing? awkward? Yes, it is all those things, but communities built around Jesus's forgiveness and healing for sin and brokenness will become safe places for people to find hope and healing. There is healing in confessing to each other because it frees us to be honest, to be real. Pretending leads only to more pain and dysfunction.

If we can be real with each other—and not just about our sins but also about our struggles and setbacks and depressions—we can help each other experience the grace of Jesus.

When we do this, we are putting skin on the reality that God himself put skin on. Jesus embraced the full experience of human frailty, all the way to the pain of death and bearing the sin of the world. He bore it all so that we would not have to bear our burdens alone. So when Christians demonstrate that we can take people's honesty, we demonstrate that God can take it too—and did. We also live out the practice of unity with one another that God so desires for us.

> If we can be real with each other, we can help each other experience the grace of Jesus.

ONE

In 1976 five teenage boys set out to accomplish what few will ever achieve: to be rock stars.

Now, to achieve rock-star status, you first have to choose a band name. This is the most important piece when you are fourteen, more important than how good the music is or even how cool you look on stage. If you have a great name, you have a chance.

The first name this new band considered was the Larry Mullen Band (suggested by the founding member and drummer), but lead singer Paul Hewson quickly axed it. Band members Paul, Dave, Dirk, Larry, and Adam agreed on the name Feedback. But by March 1977 they changed the name to the Hype. A year later, when one of the five band members was phased out, the now four-member rock band decided to change their name once again. The choice wasn't some deep epiphany that had life-impacting meaning. It was literally the one name on their brainstorming list that all four disliked the least. The new name? U2. (You may be wondering who Paul Hewson is. You know him as Bono.)

Over the past thirty-plus years, U2 has reached a pinnacle of success that very few bands will ever achieve. They are one of the most critically and commercially successful groups in popular music. The awards and accomplishments they have accumulated are staggering. U2 has cranked out twelve studio albums that have sold an impressive 150 million units. They have won twenty-two Grammys—more than any other group. And in 2005 they were inducted into the Rock and Roll Hall of Fame. Beyond the band's success, U2 and Bono have used their stage to impact the world through philanthropic efforts.

U2's rise to this level of musical dominance almost didn't happen. In 1990, just over fourteen years after U2 had started, they headed into a studio to work on a new album. There was a funk in the air, and something was pulling the band apart, fracturing their relationships. They couldn't agree on a sound for the new music. The more they worked in the studio, the more they disagreed. The more they discussed, the more divided they became. The feeling was circulating through the band that the end of U2 was inevitable.

December came, and they were still struggling in the studio. U2's guitarist, Edge, had been working on several guitar chord progressions when something amazing happened. Two chord progressions caught the attention of Bono and the rest of the band. Within fifteen minutes melodies and lyrics were forged together. The result was the song "One."

Bono describes the meaning of the song. "It is a song about coming together, but it's not the old hippie idea of

'Let's all live together.' It is, in fact, the opposite. It's saying, We are one, but we're not the same. It's not saying we even want to get along, but that we have to get along together in this world if it is to survive."[2]

"One" is considered by many to be U2's greatest song. *Rolling Stone* put it at number thirty-six of the five hundred greatest songs of all time. But beyond the outward success, it is one of the most meaningful songs to the band. So much so that the band has played "One" at every concert since the song's live debut in 1992.

Getting real with each other begins the process of becoming one. Unity is of crucial importance for Christians, not just because it is more enjoyable than division and it can bring comfort when we are torn, but also because Jesus himself specifically prayed for it. Take a look at these words from one of his last prayers before his betrayal, arrest, torture, and crucifixion:

> I am praying not only for these disciples but also for
> all who will ever believe in me through their
> message. I pray that they will all be one, just as you
> and I are one—as you are in me, Father, and I am
> in you. And may they be in us so that the world will
> believe you sent me.
> I have given them the glory you gave me, so
> they may be one as we are one. I am in them and

you are in me. May they experience such perfect
unity that the world will know that you sent me
and that you love them as much as you love me.[3]

Isn't it remarkable that, with all the anguished expectation Jesus was going through, he still took time to pray
carefully and passionately about us? With the agony of the
cross on his mind, he prayed that you and I would experience unity with each other. Why? So that we would reflect
the relationship between the Father and the Son. So that
we would be a compelling vision to those who don't believe.
So that we would become a living picture of God's love.

When we practice unity in this way—meeting together, loving each other, forgiving each other, confessing
to each other, and being radically honest with each other—
we do something extremely countercultural and extremely
attractive. People are hurting to be
known and to be accepted, even if
they don't realize it. But when they
look at the church, what do they see?
Too often they see Christians as hyp-
ocrites at worst or cliquish separatists
at best. And this vision communicates something about God. It com-
municates something false, of course, but our unity or dis-
unity will often be the only Jesus some will ever see. But if

> When we practice
> unity, we do some-
> thing extremely
> countercultural
> and extremely
> attractive.

they could see a group of God-loving people who also love each other, warts and all, they may see the God who loved us "while we were still sinners."[4]

In his classic book on community, *Life Together*, Dietrich Bonhoeffer wrote:

> The Christian needs another Christian who speaks God's Word to him. He needs him again and again when he becomes uncertain and discouraged, for by himself he cannot help himself without belying the truth. He needs his brother man as a bearer and proclaimer of the divine word of salvation. He needs his brother solely because of Jesus Christ. The Christ in his own heart is weaker than the Christ in the word of his brother; his own heart is uncertain, his brother's is sure.
>
> And that also clarifies the goal of all Christian community: they meet one another as bringers of the message of salvation.[5]

What Bonhoeffer illuminates here is our need to "good news" each other. This need presupposes, of course, that we have troubles, sins, and discouragements that are begging for good news. But we can't get to this beautiful picture of unity until we can open up enough to be honest about our sins, struggles, and setbacks.

Covering Up

In the very beginning of the biblical story, right after Adam and Eve disobeyed God by eating the forbidden fruit and ushering sin and death into the world, they realized they were naked and felt vulnerable. That started the first game of hide-and-seek. Adam and Eve tried to hide from God. They were exposed. And they didn't want God or their partner to see.[6]

This is a perfect illustration of the daunting challenge of becoming honest with God and each other. It's like getting naked. It's the deepest form of vulnerability, dating all the way back to seconds after the Fall.

Most of us carry at least two fears about sharing our pain and struggles with another person. One, we fear being exposed, being truly known by our struggles and faults, not just by the front we usually put forward. Two, we fear being rejected. Like Adam and Eve, we think that if God were to confront us in our total vulnerability, he would be appalled to the point of distancing himself from us and punishing us or shunning us.

> Becoming honest with God and each other is like getting naked. It's the deepest form of vulnerability.

So we do what Adam and Eve did. We don't just hide; we try to cover our nakedness. They did it with fig leaves.

We do it by pretending we're not hurting and putting on a happy face despite feeling dead inside. We do it by trying to make up for our faults with self-righteousness or lying to cover ourselves.

God did not accept the leaf coverings. They didn't work. But he didn't reject Adam and Eve. According to the Bible, he covered them himself using animal skins.[7] The message is vivid and clear. We can be covered, but something must die. God's providing animal skins to cover the first humans' nakedness is a picture of God's providing the sacrifice of Jesus to cover our sin.

The lesson is challenging but simple: if we want to experience the joy of unity, of relational connectedness, of the glory of God, we have to risk showing our true selves to God and others, and we have to be gracious coverers of one another with the good news of Jesus Christ's sacrifice.

The beauty of this is that the more reliable we are with grace, the more reliable our communities will be with honesty.

THE PRACTICE OF HONESTY

Getting to the place of honesty with each other can be difficult, but there are few things more rewarding—and healing. There is a divine catharsis in unburdening ourselves of sin and painful experiences. It sets us free and allows the burden to be shared, if not lifted. Why do you think they call it "getting something off your chest"?

Of course, this is a risk. It can be a disaster to fall into the hands of insensitive, insincere, or just flat-out mean Christians. Many times we are reluctant to share what's going on in our lives because we've been burned in the past by gossip, judgmentalism, bad assumptions, terrible theology, or even ambivalence or stony silence. Nevertheless, God calls us to know and be known. He wants us to be a living picture of the reconciliation he offers between himself and us. And we can't do reconciliation if we don't get real.

> There is a divine catharsis in unburdening ourselves of sin and painful experiences.

You may want to begin by identifying one Christian you can trust with the difficulties of your life. This person could be an accountability partner, an older believer whose wisdom and insight you respect, or perhaps a pastor, counselor, or therapist. Getting one on one is the first big step toward later sharing with multiple people, perhaps in a prayer group or small group or support group of some kind.

Identify cultures of grace. Are there pockets of Christians where you can see that lives have been transformed by the good news of Jesus, where sin is spoken against but sinners feel loved and cared for and not condemned? Can you see acceptance and belonging? Do you see honesty already taking place? Does the place feel warm and welcoming? Hopefully you have located this culture of grace in your own church or at least in certain groups or gatherings within your church.

When life falls apart, to some extent we all feel like we're the first to experience it. So I know that tentativeness and unease will be there regardless. But take the risk!

If you lead a small group or community group of some kind at your church, or if you work with a group of volunteers, strive to create a safe place for honesty. This probably means you will have to go first. When someone goes first, it breaks the seal of fear and discomfort that prevents transparency. When someone goes first, it immediately tells others in the group that they are not alone. And we are more likely to get honest with others when we don't feel as though we are alone. But somebody has to go first.

Will it be you?

God is faithful. He will meet you at every point with the grace you need and the healing you long for. And once you can be honest with him and find in him not rejection or condemnation but acceptance, your fear of people will gradually dissipate, giving you the confidence to get real with others too. You'll be able to let them see how you are torn, which will start helping you recover.

Check Your
Assumptions

O ne of the most paralyzing threats to trusting God with our pain may be found in our assumptions about our trials. Either consciously or unconsciously, we adopt certain perspectives about God and pain. We often assume that we are experiencing junk in our lives because of something we have done. We wonder if God is getting back at us or evening the score through our latest struggles. We listen to voices inside us and around us that condemn us. And many times our assumptions and those of others couldn't be more wrong and do untold damage to our faith and lives.

I think of the thirty-year-old woman who approached me after a weekend service. She looked as if she were carry-ing the weight of the world on her shoulders. She said, "Jud,

I have a friend at work who is going blind. All my associates are saying it's because of sin in her life. They say she's going blind because her parents sinned and made mistakes or because she's sinned and made mistakes. Can that be true?"

I was privileged to open the Bible to the scene where Jesus was walking with his disciples, and they asked him that very question after encountering a man who had been born blind:

> "Rabbi," his disciples asked him, "why was this man born blind? Was it because of his own sins or his parents' sins?"
>
> "It was not because of his sins or his parents' sins," Jesus answered. "This happened so the power of God could be seen in him."[1]

After I read this passage to her, I looked up to see tears rolling down her cheeks. She smiled and gave me the biggest bear hug.

It took me awhile to realize exactly what was going on, but at last it dawned on me. I said, "It's not your friend who's going blind, is it?"

"No," she said. "I've lost eighty percent of my vision, and the next twenty will go soon."

I said, "Let me tell you what the Bible says. This has nothing to do with specific sin in the lives of your parents or in your life. I don't know why you are facing this, but I believe you can trust God in it. God can use what you are going through to bring glory to him even in the midst of your struggle."

As she wiped the tears from her face, she was smiling from ear to ear. Now when I see her around the church, she looks like a different person. She reminds me of Jesus's words: "The truth will set you free."[2]

Wrong assumptions about God and suffering had caused her serious pain. And unfortunately these kinds of assumptions are all too real around the water coolers of our world. These falsehoods stem from and feed into our worst fears and misguided assumptions when we are suffering: Is my condition due to my specific sin? Did my parents do something wrong that I'm gonna pay for the rest of my life? Does my pain prove I'll never be forgiven by God?

Another key part of getting the *how* of suffering right, then, is making sure our assumptions about what we are going through are the right ones.

JUST HAVE MORE FAITH

My friend Janice has multiple sclerosis. She is a wonderful, godly woman, and she and her husband are two of the most spiritually mature people I know. They are amazing people of faith. But some of their friends and acquaintances have implied that if she just had more faith, she could be healed from MS. That if she only believed strongly enough, this nightmare would pass.

This prosperity gospel-ish sort of passive-aggressive spiritual blackmail has caused massive pain, and it leads to a cycle of frustration. In moments of weakness, one may think, *Maybe I* don't *have enough faith. Maybe I need to suck it up and believe more* (whatever that means). Hurting people under this sort of pressure do their best, but when things don't change, the pressure and the guilt become unbearable. Now there is spiritual pain on top of their physical or psychological pain. They have trouble trusting God because it seems like their measure of pain is directly related to their measure of belief. This places them, not God, in control. Telling people that more faith automatically results in more healing actually accomplishes the opposite of what is intended. It creates angst, distrust, and doubt.

In the case of my friend, I'm confident she has much more faith than I do! Janice's faith is strong and abounding. To imply that she only needs some vague degree of "more" to achieve healing amounts to spiritual abuse. Those of us on the consoling side of a great hurt need to realize we don't have all the answers.

Trying to be helpful, I have often cited Romans 8:28: "God causes everything to work together for the good of those who love God," a tremendous truth that has sustained millions in their difficulties through the ages. But I haven't always been sensitive to how this was heard. This passage doesn't describe the *why* behind suffering or even lessen the blow; it's more about the ultimate result. Sometimes what people hear is that what has happened is ultimately good because God will bring good out of it. But that's not what the verse says. It says God is going to work in some really horrible, painful, difficult, awful situations, and he will bring good *out* of it. This doesn't mean the situation is any less horrible.

When I lost someone close to me, I had dozens of people come along and say, "She is in a better place now." It was true, and I was thankful for their concern. Yet some of them seemed to imply that, because my friend was in heaven, I should just rejoice and move forward. I did rejoice, but I didn't simply move forward. I needed to stay awhile and grieve. I was reminded of a point made by C. S. Lewis: saying that death doesn't matter is like saying that birth doesn't matter.[3] My friend may be in a better place, but those of us who loved her have still lost something tremendous on this earth, and the pain is real. Her birth mattered, and so does her death.

When we've suffered the loss of a loved one, we need to

grieve it for what it is and take hope in heaven. In the same way, we need to be realistic about every other kind of loss or hurt.

Cause and Effect

You don't have to be a scientist to understand the law of cause and effect. You just have to have been a kid at some point in life. (I think everyone reading this book qualifies.) Kids have the law of cause and effect down to a perfected art.

If you are a parent, you have a series of questions in your arsenal that you are ready to hurl out at a moment's notice. One of the top questions you ask your kids is, "Why did you do that?" (Or "What were you thinking?") Usually the response is, "Well, _____ (fill in the name) did _____ (fill in the action) to me *first*."

Your son hauls off and hits his sister. You ask, "Why did you do that?"

He replies, "Well, she hit me first."

Your daughter defriends her best friend from Facebook. You ask, "Why did you do that?"

She replies, "Well, she told me she didn't want to be friends anymore."

Cause and effect. And it's not just for kids.

No matter how mature you feel you are, cause and effect weasels its way into your adult life. Someone cuts you off on the road (cause); what do you do in response (effect)? Your waiter messes up your order, doesn't refill your drinks, and is rude (cause); what do you tip (effect)? Your husband works late, doesn't help around the house, and plays golf way too much (cause); what do you do (effect)?

In the 2004 documentary *Super Size Me,* Morgan Spurlock set out to discover the cause and effect of fast food. The experiment was simple. He blocked out thirty days when he would eat only McDonald's fare for breakfast, lunch, and dinner. If the McDonald's employee taking his order asked if he would like to supersize anything, he would say yes. Over the next thirty days, Morgan averaged a staggering five thousand calories a day. He packed on more than twenty-four pounds and increased his body mass by 13 percent. The weight that required only thirty days to add took fourteen months to lose. Simple cause and effect. You eat five thousand calories a day, and the effect is weight gain.[4]

We often transfer this kind of thinking to God. We assume there is a law of retribution that says the righteous will prosper, but the wicked will suffer hardship. People who think in this formulaic way praise God's greatness, but they see his greatness primarily in his delivering his own from suffering. But this creates a real problem for those who are not yet delivered from their suffering or area of brokenness. They end up thinking, *If God always delivers his children from suffering, and I am suffering, does that mean I'm not a child of God? Do I need to repent of my sin?* Bad assumptions may lead us to think of our misfortunes as punishment from God, which is all the more painful when we repent and do not have our "punishment" taken away.

Jesus addressed these kinds of assumptions when he talked about a tower that fell and killed several people. He asked, "What about the eighteen people who died when the tower in Siloam fell on them? Were they the worst sinners in Jerusalem? No, and I tell you again that unless you repent, you will perish, too."[5] Jesus made it clear that tragedy and misfortune are not always because of personal sin.

Sin entered our world because of the Fall. All of us, believers and nonbelievers, face the consequences of this. Much of the evil in our world, then, is our fault, not God's. He didn't invent the electric chair or the machine gun. He didn't devise ways of torture. We did this on our own. However, he allows Satan and suffering to continue for now.

After denying that the people in Siloam died due to some specific sin, Jesus said that we should look at suffering like this and turn to God, for judgment *is* coming. The Bible speaks of a day when God will judge the world and speaks of "Christ Jesus, who is to judge the living and the dead."[6] God is coming to judge those who refuse his grace. He is continually merciful toward sinners in his good creation, and his most merciful act was sending his only Son, Jesus, to save the world from its sin. As Peter said, "The Lord is not slow to fulfill his promise as some count slowness, but is patient toward you, not wishing that any should perish, but that all should reach repentance."[7]

When we make the false and formulaic assumption that pain and suffering are always a punishment for a specific sin, we end up making the ways of God sound more like karma. Yes, there is such a thing as reaping what we sow, and there is such a thing as suffering the consequences of our actions. But the idea that all sickness and sad circumstances are the result of specific sins positions God, not as a loving Father who oversees our suffering and comforts us in it, but as an abusive Father who administers our suffering and stands over us with a hair-trigger temper. But God does not play tit for tat with his children. And the Bible flat-out says we are not destined for wrath.[8]

> When we assume that pain and suffering are always punishment for a specific sin, we end up making the ways of God sound more like karma.

GUILT TRIPPING

As we suffer, we must choose to live by faith in the revealed Word of God rather than by the assumptions of other people. It may be that we have brought our difficulty on ourselves by our actions. In these moments God may be disciplining us as his children because he loves us. But it isn't true that God is getting even for a particular sin.

Many of us believers assume we understand about God's forgiveness and grace, but when trouble comes, we often feel condemned. We assume that God's grace doesn't reach to us.

For years I lived in the odd limbo of believing in God and his grace while still feeling as though I was not forgiven. No matter what I did, I couldn't shake the sense that my past addictions and mistakes condemned me. It drove me to the performance treadmill, where I tried harder and harder to earn the love of God. When I wasn't on that treadmill, I was often wallowing in pointless guilt, because no matter how much I tried, I kept failing. And my past was always there.

> Many of us believers assume we understand about God's forgiveness and grace, but when trouble comes, we often feel condemned.

One thing I needed was to see that my refusal to accept grace was actually self-pity and pride. I had always viewed it as somehow righteous, as if I didn't fully deserve grace because of my past. But when I realized that my refusal to accept God's forgiveness was actually the height of arrogance and pride and could stir the anger of God, well, that was something else. It rattled me.

In refusing to accept grace, I was saying that my word was better than God's Word. I was saying the cross of Jesus was not enough for me. I was saying his death and sacrifice should have been greater. God had to do more in order for my sins to be forgiven. I was trapped in unhealthy guilt.

There is a difference between healthy and unhealthy guilt. Healthy guilt motivates us to mend relationships, make things right, and move toward health. It is focused more on others than on ourselves. Unhealthy guilt often results in self-hatred. We condemn ourselves. We refuse to believe we can ever be accepted.

Unhealthy guilt and shame are debilitating. I once encountered a man who was so broken from self-hatred that he was coming unglued. He said that he had prayed every day for God to forgive him for something he had done ten years earlier.

I told him to read Psalm 51, which is David's prayer for forgiveness after committing the sins of adultery, murder, lying, and covering it all up. I challenged him to read it and ask for forgiveness. Then I said, "After asking for forgiveness, don't ever ask God to forgive you for that sin again."

He was shocked and took a step back.

So I said it again, "As your pastor, I'm telling you, ask forgiveness once more, and don't ever ask God to forgive you for that sin again. He's already forgiven you. He's let it go, but you keep bringing it up every morning."

I shared with him that the Bible says, "He has removed our sins as far from us as the east is from the west."[9] The cool thing is that you can go to absolute north and south, but there is no absolute east or west. He has removed our sins from us as far as is possible. It's true that we are commanded to confess our sins, and we should do that, but let's stop bringing up the sins of old that God has already forgiven.

When we're torn, we will be tempted to doubt God's grace in many ways. So we should take heart that salvation is a gift of faith. We can't earn it, and we won't lose it due to our troubles.

> We all suffer in this messed-up world. But this doesn't mean God's grace is beyond us or unavailable to us.

We all suffer in this messed-up world. But this doesn't mean God's grace is beyond us or unavailable to us. What if we reevaluated our assumptions in light of the Bible? What if we clung to his word that there is "no condemnation for those who belong to Christ Jesus"?[10] What if we made the choice right now to let not only our expectations but also our assumptions be guided by God's Word and let our trial guide us to greater love and dependence on God?

Waiting for God

The great prophet Tom Petty reminded us that waiting is definitely the hardest part. I struggle with
waiting for much of anything, but sometimes when we are
torn, God teaches his best lessons in the waiting room. We
learn more in the valley than on the mountaintop, more in
a few hours of difficulty than we do in years of prosperity.
In the previous chapters we explored how we can share our
lives when we are torn and experience God's grace by avoiding false and misleading assumptions. Now we'll look at
some resources for the tough place of waiting on God that
all of us experience when we are torn.

Aron Ralston came face to face with the frailty of life
and an excruciating decision. He was an avid and experienced climber by the time he set out to explore Blue John
Canyon in 2003. Yet if you were to consider the top-ten list
of foolish things to do as a climber, you'd have to say that

Aron successfully accomplished all of them. Two of the biggest mistakes were that he went alone and that he didn't tell anyone where he was going.

While he was climbing, an eight-hundred-pound boulder shifted, pinning his right hand to the canyon wall. The first forty-five minutes consisted of desperate and futile attempts to hurl his body into the boulder and dislodge his hand from it. The severity of the situation quickly became apparent. Over the next six days, Aron went through every emotion you could imagine. He had hope that a search team might find him. He screamed for help, thinking that someone might, just might hear him. He begged God to do something miraculous.

God teaches his best lessons in the waiting room.

Survival was at the core of his spirit. Urine became the only substance available to keep him alive. A video camera became the tool for conveying a message to his family in case he didn't survive. Through sleepless nights and the constant mental war he was waging to live, Aron faced the one option he had hoped to avoid. He was going to have to cut off his arm if he wanted a chance to live. On the sixth day of his ordeal, he made the final decision. It was his arm or his life.

He had already spent countless hours mentally working through the best way to remove his arm—and trying to get his mind around the excruciating pain he was destined to encounter. Aron knew that, without a saw or a sharp knife, the only option was for him to break the bones in his arm. In an interview with CNN, he described it this way: "I bent my arm farther and farther, and then finally, this cracking, splintering sound, kind of like a cap gun, then, POW! It echoed up and down the canyon. I knew that I had broken my bone. And yes, it hurt. It hurt a lot."[1]

Sounds like an understatement, doesn't it? He then took a dull knife and began cutting through his flesh. Cut after painful cut, he slowly removed his arm, freeing himself from the boulder that had trapped him. When it was finished, Aron knew that what he had just done was only the beginning. He had another four hours ahead of him, climbing out of the canyon and hopefully encountering a rescue team. Aron told CNN, "I had to make a decision to go forward not knowing what was going to come. And that was important, that I took action in that moment, overcoming that fear." Aron's remarkable courage allowed him to be found. His story has been made into a major motion picture titled *127 Hours*.

It seems like every year we hear about hikers or other outdoor enthusiasts being lost in a snowstorm or in a dense wilderness. Between when they go missing and when rescuers are able to reach them, their survival often depends not on the efforts of search parties but on their own efforts.

How adept are they at building a shelter, starting a fire, staying warm, identifying edible vegetation? How resilient are they? How hopeful are they? The key to staying alive for those who get desperately lost is not knowing how to be found but knowing how to survive until they are found.

Sometimes the faith journey feels a lot like this. You're stuck, you're waiting, and you desperately long to be found. One of the hardest parts of waiting is the loneliness that creeps into your life. You can even feel lonely for God.

DARK NIGHT OF THE SOUL

Have you ever heard of the dark night of the soul? No, this isn't a reference to Batman—that's the dark *knight*—but rather to an intense period of loneliness and emotional desolation, a sort of spiritual depression that may leave sufferers despairing of life itself. For many Christians, the dark night of the soul is a good description of the times in their lives when God has felt impossibly distant and depressingly silent. At one time in my life, I spent several years in this darkness and wondered where God was. I kept serving him, but I didn't sense him.

The phrase "the dark night of the soul" comes from a sixteenth-century Christian mystic. St. John of the Cross was born in 1542 in Fontiveros, Spain, and entered the priesthood as an adult. After his reform attempts inside the

Catholic Church failed, he was taken captive by his superiors and imprisoned. He was banished to a small room with nothing but bread and water. He was beaten and left to suffer alone in a cell that, depending on the weather, could be extremely hot or extremely cold. He languished there for almost a year.

Eventually he escaped his captors and found refuge with a group of nuns. This is when he wrote the classic spiritual work *Dark Night of the Soul*. The book (which is actually a poem) describes in detail how God can use suffering to draw us closer to him. It begins by describing the first purification of suffering, called the dark night of the senses. Later in the book we learn of the second purification, the dark night of the spirit. Each of these dry and desperate times in one's spiritual walk, according to his poetic writings, results in more perfect communion with God.

> For many Christians, the dark night of the soul is a good description of the times in their lives when God has felt impossibly distant and depressingly silent.

I know this all sounds like some weird kind of emo pop lyrics, but he really was talking about some spiritually heavy stuff. This stuff is way above Death Cab for Cutie's pay grade.

The author described how we need the dark night of the senses. As believers, we are moved by the pleasure we find in spiritual activities: prayer, meditation, and service. And yet all of us have many imperfections and are in need of God's purifying ways. St. John of the Cross described each of the seven fundamental sins that grip us: pride, greed, luxury, anger, gluttony, envy, and laziness. The dark night we go through can destroy much of the power of these sins.

How do we know if we are experiencing the dark night of the senses? According to him, we find no pleasure or consolation in the things of God, even though we once did. We start to think we're not serving God and are backsliding. Our ability to meditate on the goodness of God around us dissipates. Where the heavens might have once declared the glory of God to us, where certain smells or sounds or sights might have tuned in our sense of worship, the senses now seem cut off to any spiritual frequency.

It is in this time that many people feel forsaken by God. They grow weary and feel as though they have failed. He challenges us to wait on God in the trial and be patient. God is leading us down a new path and will ultimately bring us to peace and quietness.

St. John of the Cross further explained the benefits of the night of the senses. In our suffering we come to know ourselves more fully. We become aware of how unworthy we are in comparison to God. We learn to relate to him with more respect and more courtesy. Overall, because of the difficulty, we find pleasure in doing things for God's glory and not our own. Even in this pain, God is renewing us through his light. We may not know that this is happening, but God is creating a more complete union between us and him.

One of the hardest but sweetest truths of the spiritual life is this: God humbles his children in order to exalt them. He strips away everything else and replaces it with himself in order for us to experience the fullness of all things. When the only source of hope is God himself, we can learn again what it means to have the joy of the Lord as our strength. And ultimately, in this process of having everything stripped away but the essence of our salvation, we find freedom.

> Ultimately, in the process of having everything stripped away but the essence of our salvation, we find freedom.

St. John of the Cross described the dark times with the metaphor of wood and fire. In the beginning, fire dries out the wood. It begins to make it black and dark and even gives it a bad odor. The flame dries it out a little at a time until it drives away the dark. Finally it begins to kindle a big flame and give off heat. It produces a fire. In our lives God allows the dryness and darkness so that they will produce an intense fire and passion for God alone.

The life story of St. John of the Cross clearly displays the trials that God put him through. He suffered loss, rejection, imprisonment, failing health, and torment. Although he never specifically calls the night "depression," we can infer that he was brought low.

I want to make two points here. One, he assumed that all Christians will suffer to some degree. He reminded us that to follow Christ is to lay down our lives. And God will allow pain, even great pain, to bring about the transformation of his people. God delights in transforming his people, in ridding them of sin. Second, according to St. John of the Cross, this experience is actually a privilege and a way to become more connected to Christ. He pointed out the deep pain that was caused by these nights, and yet he reminded us of how magnificent it is to be united to Christ. The journey may be difficult and full of suffering, but it is the way to God.

We learn from St. John of the Cross that we should not be surprised when God allows suffering in our lives. We should not be ashamed if at some point in the Christian life we experience dark and difficult seasons. Maybe you feel torn right now and you don't know why. Trust that God is at work in your life to accomplish awesome things, even in the dry seasons.

HOPE IN THE WAITING

Four words make up the dreaded phrase on every family vacation since Adam and Eve had kids. (Okay, I might not be able to prove that, but you have to assume it's true.) It is the phrase that can go on for miles without an answer to satisfy the questioning mind. No matter what method of transportation you are using, and no matter at what speed you are moving, it will be relentlessly uttered. It is a phrase that every kid (yes, even you at one time) has said. A phrase that will be repeated until the world comes to an end. The phrase is, "Are we there yet?" And as soon as that phrase comes rolling off the lips of every kid in the car (or plane, or boat, or wagon), the next dreaded phrase comes rushing out as if to send your brain into overload. "How much longer?" The first time or even the fifth time these two phrases are uttered, you give a kind and compassionate answer. But there is a magical number after which the answers become cold, calculating, and sarcastic.

Here's the thing, though. As adults, we're not much different. We might have more patience in waiting for our car trip destination, but when it comes to being torn, we can't help asking again and again how much longer we'll have to put up with it.

I love the way the book of Psalms in the Bible captures the whole range of human existence. There is basically no feeling or frailty you can think of that isn't at least mentioned in one of the psalms. What we get in David's psalms, in particular, is an honest crying out to God about feelings of despair, abandonment, longing, pain, and even waiting.

David is a guy who was often afflicted by his past and was in over his head in the present. Many times he cried out to God, asking, "How long?"

"How long will I have to endure this pain?"

"How long will I have to face this uncertainty?"

"How long will others make my life miserable?"

"How long will I have to deal with this hurt?"

Maybe you've asked these questions of God. Sometimes we think our hurt would be bearable if only it didn't last so darn long! Or we get through one problem only to be faced with another and then another. The hits just keep on coming. And, exhausted and exasperated, we pray, "God, how much longer is this going to last?"

Take a look at the opening lines from David's Psalm 69:

Save me, O God,
>for the floodwaters are up to my neck.
Deeper and deeper I sink into the mire;
>I can't find a foothold.
I am in deep water,
>and the floods overwhelm me.
I am exhausted from crying for help;
>my throat is parched.
My eyes are swollen with weeping,
>waiting for my God to help me.[2]

David felt so overwhelmed that it was as if he were drowning. And he couldn't even cry for help anymore—he was too tired, and his throat was parched from the crying anyway. He was worn-out from the waiting.

Yet David was still able to confess to God, "Your unfailing love is wonderful" (verse 16). How did he do that? How did he go from drowning one moment to declaring that the very seas will praise God the next?[3]

The answer lies with David's hope. He may have been drowning, but he knew who controls the seas. Time may have been running long on his unmet hopes and expectations, but he knew the God who stands outside of time and who loved him before time began.

> Many times what may feel like dry periods of waiting are really God's means of preparation.

This insight makes it all the more important not to try to pinpoint what God is doing based purely on what we're experiencing or feeling. His ways are not ours. Many times what may feel like dry periods of waiting are really his means of preparation. Andrew Murray, the nineteenth-century South African pastor and author, wrote:

We ought to make up our minds to this, that nothing was ever so sure, as that waiting on God will bring us untold and unexpected blessing. We are so accustomed to judge of God and His work in us by what we feel, that the great probability is that when we begin more to cultivate the waiting on Him, we shall be discouraged, because we do not find any special blessing from it. The message comes to us, "Above everything, when you wait on God, do so in the spirit of abounding hopefulness. It is God in His glory, in His power, in His love longing to bless you that you are waiting on."

If you say that you are afraid of deceiving yourself with vain hope, because you do not see or feel any warrant in your present state for such special expectations, my answer is, it is God, who is the warrant for your expecting great things.[4]

Memory

What do we do if we are waiting on God and going through a dark period or even our own dark night of the soul? One important thing we can do is *remember*. When I go through difficult times, I often forget the blessing. I focus on the challenges around me and forget all that God did for me when the sun was shining on my face.

In the Bible we read how God told the Israelites again and again to remember what he had done for them. They were to remember how he brought them out of Egypt and defeated the Egyptians who were seeking to enslave them. They were to remember God's gracious dealings with them in the wilderness, his provision for survival, for victory, for justice, for worship, and for relational intimacy with him and each other. They were to recall the covenant he had made with his people through Abraham. God urged his people to remember all these things so they would have ready historical references to his faithfulness in their times of fear, uncertainty, and doubt.

Without memory, human life is not possible in the way we know it. Only by remembering do we add thickness to our lives. I heard of a man who, because of a trauma suffered in World War II, has had only five-minute short-term recall for anything occurring to him since then. He is constantly reinventing reality. Every face he meets is a new face, even the ones of those who care for him daily. Every experience is a new experience. Could there be a worse fate than continually being cut off from one's own experience, retaining nothing, building on nothing, relating to nothing? Our memories bind our life together.

Be assured, God has created your brain in a magnificent way to retain the memories in your life. There is no way your mind will run out of space to store information. Paul Reber, professor of psychology at Northwestern University, was asked these questions: "What is the memory capacity of the human brain? Is there a physical limit to the amount of information it can store?"

Dr. Reber replied,

> The human brain consists of about one billion neurons.... Neurons combine..., exponentially increasing the brain's memory storage capacity to something...around 2.5 petabytes... For comparison, if your brain worked like a digital video recorder in a television, 2.5 petabytes would be enough to hold three million hours of TV shows.[5]

Our capacity is incredible. (But this does make me wonder why I'm always forgetting where I put my car keys!)

We're called to flex our amazing mental potential and remember that God has not abandoned us in the past, and he has promised he will never do so in the future.[6] The past provides a concrete expression of God's unchanging love for us to hold on to. We can always look back and remember how God brought us from our personal captivity into his rest. We can recall God's past answers to our prayers and find assurance that the invisible reality in which we place our hope and trust has been revealed in our lives.

A reporter once asked Supreme Court Chief Justice Earl Warren if it was true he always read the sports page of the newspaper first. Warren replied, "The sports pages report men's triumphs and the front page seems always to be reporting their failures. I prefer to read about men's triumphs rather than their failures."[7]

Think about when God was faithful to you. When you felt close to him, full of love and full of joy. Remember when you felt as though he was blessing your socks off. Remember God's faithfulness in your time of pain. The truth is that God is always nearby, that God is always blessing you, that God is never being unfaithful to you. So stop turning to the front-page news of your life and instead turn to the sports section and reflect on the triumphs.

> We're called to remember that God has not abandoned us in the past, and he has promised he will never do so in the future.

When we go through a time of darkness, it's important to remember the light of God in our past. We don't remember merely God's handling of our pain in the past but God's *inhabiting* our pain, God's experiencing our pain at the cross.

REMEMBER THE CROSS

People often think God is mostly present in the big, obvious, and ostentatious things of life: the beauty of nature, impressive church architecture, and magnificent monuments to faith. But the New Testament tells us something practically incomprehensible, totally unexpected, and consistently scandalous. If you're looking for God, you will find him hanging on a cross, bloodied and broken. You will see him in a tortured, dying man wondering where his Father is. Theologians have called this irony the scandal of the cross. Looking for God, you will find him dead—only to find him alive again three days later. He hangs there between two other executed people, suffering with them, not singing like the satirical substitutes in Monty Python's *Life of Brian,* "Always look on the bright side of life," but rather crying out in pain and in victory, "It is finished!"

That's where God is, and that's what God does.

The cross can give us hope in our darkest hour. In Psalm 22, David cried out, "My God, my God, why have you abandoned me? Why are you so far away when I groan for help?"[8] This psalm records David's expression of the trembling depths of his sorrow, but it also records his return to hope. Deliverance from sorrow will be found in *remembering* God's good deeds: "All the ends of the earth will remember and turn to the LORD, and all the families of the nations will bow down before him, for dominion belongs to the LORD and he rules over the nations."[9]

David was not alone in feeling forsaken by God. Jesus Christ, God incarnate, echoed the very words spoken by David when he said, "My God, my God, why have you abandoned me?"[10] On the cross, Jesus Christ identified with human suffering not only by bearing the sins of the world but also by suffering alongside those who are guilty. The glorious Son humbled himself and became man so he could become like the anguished, the bitter, and the broken. By quoting Psalm 22, he uttered the cry that millions before and after him have lifted to the heavens. He also expressed confidence in the One who could save him from pain: God, who has saved in the past and is able to save now (even though all signs may indicate reason for despair). This tension is nothing less than the tension of faith, and Jesus's faith is perfect.

> The glorious Son humbled himself and became man so he could become like the anguished, the bitter, and the broken.

In our moments of pain and sorrow, in our temptations and trials, we can find extraordinary, supernatural comfort in the historical fact that God inhabited the ordinary, natural world in the person of Jesus. He was tempted and subjected to suffering as we are, and he died the death for sin that we deserve. According to the prophet Isaiah, by his wounds we are healed.[11]

Comfort

In the waiting we can find hope in remembering all that God has done. Meanwhile, we can find comfort in several places:

In community. As we have seen, nothing can be so isolating as pain. Even when we are surrounded by caretakers, our pain draws us into ourselves, makes us attentive only to ourselves. Because of this, our suffering may make us feel alone even when we are not. We may have trouble experiencing God's nearness as well as the nearness of others, and we may even push away those who are attempting to help. But God has designed us to be relational people. He has wired us to share each other's burdens. Community brings a togetherness to situations even when everything is falling apart.

In solitude. As important as community is, sometimes aloneness in our times of trouble provides an opportunity for us to reflect. Alone time can be important as we process our difficult experiences, and we need to be wise enough to discern when community is appropriate and when withdrawal is appropriate. Seek wisdom to know the balance between processing your hurts alone with God and dwelling needlessly on your pain. To be sure, being alone while drifting toward despair is not a good thing, but sometimes getting alone and *feeling* and then hashing out our feelings with God is a vital part of the journey out of a dark period.

In expression. Everyone needs to express his hurts in some way. This may take the form of grieving words, aching prayers, or other art forms that express the recesses of the soul. You may try journaling or keeping a diary to express your thoughts. Your cathartic expression could be anything from the formalized painting of a picture to just locking yourself in your room, cranking up some tunes, and singing along loudly. Whatever helps you express your hurts can be helpful in journeying through them. I crank up my Gibson Les Paul Goldtop guitar through a Bad Cat amp and let the neighbors in on it!

In memorial. For many, it is important to establish regular memorials in honor of those who have passed. The Jewish tradition has a healthy practice in which, on the first anniversary of the death of a parent or other close family member, a child is instructed to memorialize the dead and say prayers. Many people place flowers on graves every year (in East Asia they sweep the graves) or perform some other practices that help the grieving work through their loss.

In Scripture. While the words of the Bible may not solve a problem immediately for someone in the midst of suffering, they can be the greatest help. The Scriptures record God's words to his people, his actions on their behalf, and his commitments to do good for and to his children.

The Bible is filled with the raw, honest thoughts and feelings of many people who suffered greatly and trusted God. If you are desperate for the calming voice of God in the storms of your life, there is no better resource for you than the Bible, which reveals God's very words.

UNASHAMED

In the movie *The Edge*, Anthony Hopkins gets lost in the deep woods of Alaska and finds himself being stalked by both a killer grizzly bear and Alec Baldwin. Can you imagine a ferocious hairy beast breathing down your neck? (And that bear would have to be scary too.) At one point in the film, Hopkins's character, who is a bit of a bookworm and trivia buff, says to his companions before they are picked off by the bear, "I once read an interesting book which said that most people lost in the wilds...die of shame."[12]

When our world is rocked, we can feel lost just waiting on God to begin our healing. It can be like a kid lost in the woods. It's dark and dangerous. The trees are dense. The environment is not familiar. We feel alone, exposed. Maybe abandoned.

Most people who die in the woods die of shame. They hunker down in a hole and despair.

If you're lost in the woods, you don't have to do that. If you're waiting on God—and waiting and waiting and waiting—you don't have to despair. In the psalms David wrote, "None who wait for you shall be put to shame."[13] You may not know why this has happened to you, but there is no shame in waiting for him. In fact, by dwelling with God in the wilderness, we are marked by him as his. And all who are called by God and covered by his grace have no need to be ashamed.

Think of all the people in the Bible who waited a long time for deliverance. Joseph is one. Moses is another. Paul is a third. The entire nation of Israel is a great example! And yet all were rewarded in God's time

> You may not know why this has happened to you, but there is no shame in waiting for God.

and in God's way. They may not have received exactly what they expected, but at last they got what they really longed for, and in Christ their hopes were not put to shame.

While you wait for God, do not be ashamed to hurt. Be confident that he loves you, and be hopeful that deliverance is coming.

As the Bible says, "It is no shame to suffer for being a Christian. Praise God for the privilege of being called by his name!"[14]

Fight for Joy

Years ago my wife, Lori, and I, along with our then six-month-old daughter, moved away from friends and extended family in Texas and headed to California. I had taken a ministry job and was excited by the new challenges. About a year after we moved, though, I noticed that Lori was acting differently. She wasn't going out much anymore, wasn't interacting with friends, and in many ways appeared to be hibernating. I should have seen it sooner, but in the frantic pace of life, I missed it. When it finally dawned on me that she was really struggling, she had already been in a deep depression for months. Her slide into depression was so slow and gradual that even she didn't fully understand what was happening.

Eventually Lori went to a doctor and told him what she was feeling. He listened and immediately prescribed depression medication. This really upset her, but not because we think people shouldn't use medicine to treat depression. They should. No, it bothered her that this person listened to her talk for no more than ten minutes and gave her a prescription. She didn't feel like she had really been heard and thought the prescription was just a quick move to get on to the next client. Something about coming home with that piece of paper, though, made the depression real for her.

We went for a walk after the appointment. As we talked, a torrent of thoughts and feelings came gushing out of my wife. She had been so concerned that I do well in my new job and that our family do well in our new home that she had refused to admit her struggles. Having moved away from longtime friends, she found building new friendships a bigger challenge than she had expected. She missed home and family. Yet she had felt a need to gloss over her disappointments, bottle up her feelings, and pretend that everything was fine. We walked for a long time, and it all came out.

Today she says that was the day her depression began to break. It wasn't all sunny skies thereafter. She wasn't singing with Ren and Stimpy, "Happy, happy, joy, joy" by the weekend. But that was the day she stopped pretending and began the long climb out of the pit she'd slid into.

In the course of this book so far, we've touched on depression briefly a few times. But now let's look at it more closely and consider the importance of facing depression and dealing with it in a healthy way. Depression can be a side effect of other kinds of suffering as well as a form of suffering in itself. Many will face it at one level or another when torn.

Depression is a big problem. Statistics show that it affects approximately nineteen million Americans in any given one-year period. "At some point in their lives, 10%–25% of women and 5%–12% of men will likely become clinically depressed."[1] Depression knows no ethnic, socioeconomic, gender, or national boundaries. Depression can be triggered by outward events or circumstances. But it doesn't need outside trouble to occur; it sometimes creeps up on people slowly and without warning.

> Oddly, sometimes in the church we explicitly or implicitly suggest to others that, if everything is not fine, then pretending it's fine is an acceptable substitute.

Oddly, sometimes in the church we explicitly or implicitly suggest to others that, if everything is not fine, then pretending it's fine is an acceptable substitute. We create a culture where Christians feel as if they have to stuff all their emotions and paint a smile over them. For all our celebration of the truth and honest living, we tend to cultivate inauthentic lives by making our communities unsafe for transparency.

Maybe you feel as though you have to pretend too.

Maybe your friends or family have made it seem inconvenient or too messy for you to be honest about what you're going through. Or maybe it's just a pressure you're putting on yourself.

I'm here to tell you that it's okay, no, necessary to admit how bad you're feeling. And I'm going to tell you something both my wife and I have learned: joy is something you have to choose and fight for. Not timidly, but boldly, like Russell Crowe in *Gladiator*.

A Common Struggle

Consider the life of Charles Haddon Spurgeon, one of the greatest pastors and communicators of the nineteenth century. At fifteen Spurgeon came to know Christ, and just four years after his conversion, he became the pastor of London's New Park Street Chapel, which later became the Metropolitan Tabernacle. He remained their faithful pastor for thirty-eight years. (In many ways Spurgeon has been my pastor through his writings. The dude can bring it!)

On January 8, 1856, he married Susannah Thompson. That same year he would endure one of the most horrific events of his lifetime. He was preaching in the Music Hall of the Royal Surrey Gardens to thousands of people when someone yelled, "Fire!" There was no fire, but seven people were killed, and many more were injured, trampled in the chaos. Nine years after the Surrey Gardens tragedy, Susannah became an invalid and was unable to leave their home and hear her husband speak for the next twenty-seven years.

In addition, Spurgeon endured pain. Not the "I stubbed my toe on the coffee table" kind of stuff, but real pain. He suffered from gout, rheumatism, and Bright's disease (a kidney condition). His first attack of illness came in 1869, when he was thirty-five years old. His pain increasingly worsened. He dealt with vomiting, fever, swelling, and mental exhaustion.

For more than half of his ministry, Spurgeon struggled with these physical and emotional ailments. (And I think I have it bad when the Dallas Cowboys lose!)

He also faced public criticism. His contemporaries accused him of being unpolished and uncouth because he had no formal education or training. But the criticism reached its peak during the Downgrade Controversy. In October 1887 he withdrew from the Baptist Union, believing that they were supporting false teaching in their denials of the truth of the Bible. Because of his strong stand, he was officially censured by the union. (If the Internet had existed back then, can you imagine what the bloggers would have written about him?)

But on top of everything else, Spurgeon wrestled with

depression. One of his first encounters with it was in 1858, at twenty-four years of age, and he would struggle with it for the rest of his life. He described the experience this way: "My spirits were sunken so low that I could weep by the hour like a child, and yet I knew not what I wept for."[2] Anyone familiar with depression knows that inexplicable sadness and crying are common.

The amazing thing about Spurgeon is that he kept functioning. By faith, he kept pushing through in spite of his depression. He said,

> I am the subject of depressions of spirit so fearful that
> I hope none of you ever get to such extremes of
> wretchedness as I go to, but I always get back again
> by this—I know I trust Christ. I have no reliance but
> in him, and if he falls I shall fall with him, but if he
> does not, I shall not. Because he lives, I shall live also,
> and I spring to my legs again and fight with my
> depressions of spirit and my downcastings, and get
> the victory through it; and so may you do, and so
> you *must,* for there is no other way of escaping from
> it. In your most depressed seasons you are to get joy
> and peace through believing.… Do stick to this, dear
> friends, "Though he slay me, yet will I trust in him."[3]

Those last words are from the book of Job.[4]

Spurgeon saw his suffering as part of God's greater plan for good. He was able to encourage the downcast, the brokenhearted, the faint, the weak, and the sick because he personally dealt with similar trials. How many people were helped and encouraged in their faith because of Spurgeon's life of hardship! He wrote, "I am afraid that all the grace that I have got of my comfortable and easy times and happy hours, might almost lie on a penny. But the good that I have received from my sorrows, and pains, and griefs, is altogether incalculable.... Affliction is the best bit of furniture in my house."

> The cloud is black before it breaks, and overshadows before it yields its deluge of mercy.

Not only did his affliction lead to his greater impact, but he also learned that there was a spiritual aspect to it. As he put it, "This depression comes over me whenever the Lord is preparing a larger blessing for my ministry; the cloud is black before it breaks, and overshadows before it yields its deluge of mercy. Depression has now become to me as a prophet in rough clothing, a John the Baptist, heralding the nearer coming of my Lord's richer benison."[5]

Have you ever thought that your depression could be preparing you for something greater? Maybe the struggle in your life is really God getting you ready for greater blessing.

The Reality of Depression

Depression touches the entire person. When those who struggle are emotionally low, often their bodies react. They are sluggish and sleep more than normal. They have a loss of appetite, loss of interest, and difficulty concentrating. The body is so closely tied to the mind and soul that it is hard to separate one from the other. But research shows over and over that the chemicals in the body affect the processes of the brain. The enzymes that help transfer the electrical energy in the brain seem to be lower during depression and higher when the depression lifts. This suggests that during depression the transmission of electrical energy is much lower. Thus the benefit of enzyme-enhancing medication appears obvious.[6]

Because of the biochemical reality behind most kinds of depression, to say that depression is all spiritual or all psychological or all physical is too simplistic. Elizabeth Ruth Skoglund wrote, "A person's body, mind, and spirit make up a totality in which one or the other may emerge predominately at any given time. A woman going through menopause may experience periods of depression that should not be labeled as primarily psychological or spiritual. She may derive help from spiritual or psychological sources, but the primary cause is physical. Certain drugs are now being used effectively with some forms of mental illness, further validating the biochemical basis for many emotional problems."[7]

Many Christians wonder if it is okay to take medicine or to see a doctor for depression. They may talk about other struggles in their lives, but they often feel shame and embarrassment about their depression. Well-meaning but ill-informed Christians can create more hurt or struggles in others by suggesting that to take medication for depression or mental disorders is to distrust God.

There is no chapter and verse that can prove a biblical case for medicine or antidepressants. But knowing that God is in the business of restoring all of creation helps us to see how medicine is a common grace in pushing back the curse of Genesis 3. Furthermore, the Bible says, "A merry heart does good, like medicine," which implies that medicine is good.[8]

> To deny someone advancements in medical technology for some sentimentally spiritual reason makes about as much sense as telling nearsighted people not to wear glasses.

Certainly the use of antidepressants ought to be seen as an issue of Christian freedom. It is a matter of conscience and conviction for those who struggle and a matter of discussion between them and their doctors, perhaps even their pastors. But to deny someone advancements in medical technology that can be of great relief for some sentimentally spiritual reason makes about as much sense as telling nearsighted people not to wear glasses or heart patients not to take blood pressure medication. God has gifted people with the wisdom to create helps for physical and emotional ailments, and as long as these helps are not forbidden by Scripture or the law of the land, we should trust that God has given us the wisdom to know whether to use them or not.

In most cases antidepressants don't change people's mood but rather correct chemical imbalances that allow sufferers to feel happy and sad at appropriate times, to take control of their emotions. Most of those who suffer from depression don't want artificial sedation to forget their troubles. They desire a sense of normalcy, an ability to process their troubles and manage their emotional reactions the same as everyone else does.

FRUSTRATED GIANTS

Like Spurgeon, many of those who were used by God in biblical times struggled with depression. As Job waited on God in his grief, he no doubt experienced depression. Jonah felt defeated after God did not fulfill the threat to destroy Nineveh. Jeremiah wished that he had never been born. David cried out in the middle of his suffering, "My tears have been my food day and night.... Why are you downcast, O my soul? Why so disturbed within me?"[9] Elijah felt hopeless at one point and even wanted to die.

In 1 Kings 18–19 we see that Elijah confronted Ahab, the king of Israel, for allowing Baal worship in Israel. On Mount Carmel, Elijah demonstrated the Lord's power by asking him to send down fire to consume the burnt offering. The prophets of Baal had tried to do the equivalent and had failed, exposing their god as a fraud. God answered Elijah's prayer and sent fire to consume the offering. This was huge—bigger than the Cubs going to the World Series. God showed up in a cosmic way!

After Elijah witnessed this victory, he hoped that his battle with Baal worship was finished. But it wasn't. Ahab's wife, Jezebel, threatened Elijah's life. So he escaped by traveling as far away as he could get. In fact, he went about 120 miles, which would have taken him around six days on foot. The physical suffering alone was enough to bring him to the bottom. He was hungry and thirsty and weak from the travel. As he entered the wilderness and sat down, exhausted, under a broom tree, he said, "It is enough; now, O LORD, take away my life, for I am no better than my fathers."[10]

Elijah was so emotionally distraught and physically drained that he asked the Lord to take his life. He saw no reason to continue; he was overcome with feelings of failure and helplessness. Even after he had called down fire from heaven, the hearts of the people were still hardened toward God. How could he have witnessed this amazingly powerful miracle and not seen results? It was enough to prompt Elijah to wonder if God was really at work after all. Elijah's work, and all the suffering he had endured because of his work, seemed to have been for nothing. He had arrived at rock bottom.

Yet God intervened to preserve and encourage Elijah. He sent an angel to give him food and nourishment so that he was able to persevere for the rest of the journey. After he was physically revived, Elijah was reminded that God was still in control despite the apparent failure of Elijah's mission.

> Elijah might have been looking for explosive power, but God was showing him that he was in the thin silences of life as well.

When Elijah came to a cave to rest, God told him to go to the mountain and stand before him. A strong wind blew, and an earthquake rumbled, and a fire burned, but the Lord was not in any of these things. He came to Elijah in a whisper. The Hebrew word for "whisper" means "a voice/sound, a thin silence."[11] Elijah had experienced a spiritual high on Mount Carmel. Coming down from that experience to the wilderness and the reality that his life was in danger was sobering. Elijah had forgotten that, although God does reveal himself in big moments, he also reveals himself in the quiet. Elijah might have been looking for explosive power, but God was showing him that he was in the thin silences of life as well. He had not forgotten Elijah or the people of God. And his plans, which were not so obvious to Elijah, were in fact being accomplished.

Even at his lowest point, Elijah learned to bring his suffering and pain to God. He came to understand that these painful moments in his life were merely chapters in a greater story, and this greater story doesn't end with suffering. He believed the promises of God would one day be fulfilled. His hope for joy in the Lord was revived.

The Right Moves

Where are you looking for joy or happiness? Do you think there is a magical formula that will make you happy? Do you think that if you lose ten more pounds or achieve six-pack abs, you will experience happiness? Or maybe for you it is finding your soul mate. Or if Stephenie Meyer writes more in the Twilight series (please, no!).

For a lot of people, it's about the almighty dollar. You may think you'll be happy if you get one more pay raise or that new position. Better yet, if you hit the lottery jackpot, then happiness will fill your life. You even pray over the numbers before picking them, extending a quick bribe toward heaven: "God, if you make it possible for me to win,

I will give twenty percent—no, thirty percent—of my winnings to the church." But just having more money without having concrete things to ground your life and provide you with joy will likely lead to frustration. More stuff means more to worry about, more to protect, and more to distract yourself with if you are not grounded. And it will never be enough.

What are you searching after to create joy in your life?

For some Christians, it is easy to find joy. For many others, finding happiness or joy is a herculean effort. If you are torn, fight tooth and nail for joy in God. The Bible indicates that joy is something we choose as much as it is something that happens to us. The Scriptures command us to rejoice throughout. One example is Paul's urging in the emphatic Philippians 4:4: "Always be full of joy in the Lord. I say it again—rejoice!"

> Joy is something we choose as much as it is something that happens to us.

But how do we do that? When the world seems to be crumbling around us, how do we choose joy? Still more, how are we to "be full"? It sounds as though the command is to do something that happens to us, to be active about something that is essentially passive. How is that possible?

You can experience this filling by simply remaining open to the work of God. Only the Spirit can make your joy full, but you can stay open to this filling by creating conditions in your life that are best used by the Spirit. Creating these conditions can consist of anything from improving your diet and getting regular exercise (which has been proven to facilitate mental and emotional health as much as physical health) to getting regular exposure to sunshine. Adopt a new hobby—or a new pet! If you have a chemical imbalance, then be faithful in taking your medications and following your doctor's instructions. Most important, regularly ask God in prayer to restore your joy.

All this is part of having the right moves in your battle against depression. After all, if you're gonna get into a fight, you'd better know some moves, or you'll get whipped. It makes no sense to try fighting for joy if you don't know the right posture and position.

At times we need to constantly war with our attitude in fighting for joy. The Bible says, "Fix your thoughts on what is true, and honorable, and right, and pure, and lovely, and admirable. Think about things that are excellent and worthy of praise."[12] Let's break it down:

Whatever is true. Things may not be going well for you, and it is okay to admit it, but also admit that God is good and he isn't finished yet. This is true too. God's Word reminds us that we live in a fallen world where things are really hard, but we also have the hope of God in our lives.

Whatever is honorable. This word is used in the Bible to refer to the lifestyles of leaders in the church, honest people who are worthy of being looked up to. Think of the good people who are making a difference in the world. I think of Tony Dungy and Billy Graham. I think of the thousands of people who are volunteering their time to make a difference in people's lives all around the world.

Whatever is right. Right and *righteous* speak of good moral choices. Consider the things in your world and your life that are right. For me, this means being selective when I watch the news, because they are always showing stories of what is wrong in the world!

Whatever is pure. Clean thoughts are possible. I think about the laughter of my kids, the sacrifice that Jesus made for me, the awesome sight of someone being baptized and taking spiritual steps.

Whatever is lovely. Beauty is found everywhere, even in brokenness. To me, everything from great music (classic rock, independent artists, basically anything but country!) to a wonderful book is lovely. Check out the sunrise with a grande dry cappuccino in the cool of the morning—now that is lovely!

Whatever is admirable. This literally means "of good reputation." What is admirable in your life or neighborhood? I see people serving the poor, being less selfish, reaching out to help their neighbors.

Whatever is excellent or praiseworthy. In the 1980s people said "excellent" after just about everything. Okay, parachute pants and big hair bands may not have been excellent, but Pat Benatar surely was. Focus on the stuff that is excellent about your life. If you can't think of anything, visit the hospital and walk the floor; that always reminds me that I have a lot to be thankful for.

Identify everything that is good in life and then "think about such things." This literally means to dwell on them. It is so easy to continually dwell on the negative or to perpetually fill our minds with worry, but if we are going to realize God's peace, then it will mean filling our thoughts with positive things. This is not wearing rose-colored glasses or sugarcoating the truth but rather making a real effort to focus on the good stuff and trust God. As the Bible says, "Watch over your heart with all diligence, for from it flow the springs of life."[13] What we focus on and dwell on flows out into everything in our lives. I'm seeking to let faith and peace push away fear and anxiety.

> What we focus on flows out into everything in our lives.

In his great book *Spiritual Depression,* David Martyn Lloyd-Jones described going through trials as being put in God's gymnasium. He wrote:

> I defy you to read the life of any saint that has ever adorned the life of the Church without seeing at once that the greatest characteristic in the life of

that saint was discipline and order. Invariably it is the universal characteristic of all the outstanding men and women of God. Read about Henry Martyn, David Brainerd, Jonathan Edwards, the brothers Wesley, and Whitfield—read their journals. It does not matter what branch of the Church they belonged to, they have all disciplined their lives and have insisted upon the need for this; and obviously it is something that is thoroughly scriptural and absolutely essential. "For he that cometh unto God must believe that He is," says the author of the Epistle to the Hebrews (11.6), yes, and also "that He is a rewarder of them that diligently seek Him." We must be diligent in our seeking.[14]

In the midst of trouble, there will be no benefit in reverting to self-pity and wallowing. You can't control what happens to you, but you can control how you react to it. Don't let life pass you by. Engage it, even if it is bringing pain. With the right moves, you can fight for joy.

THE OPEN DOOR

In *A Grief Observed,* C. S. Lewis spoke of the problems posed by his inescapable grief after his wife's death. He felt that God had slammed a door in his face, and when he prayed, he heard nothing back but silence. He discovered that when he was alone, he felt his grief more than ever and wanted to be in the presence of people with whom he might find comfort. However, once he was around other people, he wanted to be alone. He mulled over several reasons for this predicament.

When he came into contact with a person who knew about his wife's death, he often encountered a hand extended in kindness. But this expression of love made him feel angry at times, because he knew that none of the experiences in that person's life could be aligned with his deep suffering. They were offering sympathy, not empathy, and their lack of continuity with Lewis's grief made their words seem trite and irrelevant.

Some people would sense Lewis's anguish and avoid speaking of the loss of his wife altogether. This also made him angry, for he felt as if every word offered to him was merely tiptoeing around the elephant in the room. This, in turn, reminded him of his anguish all the more and provided no comfort to him.

Then there were those who were silent with Lewis. These people provided some measure of comfort, but he felt that their silence revealed the incomprehensible depth of his own suffering, so even this failed to console him.

Lewis concluded that no one could do anything to help him, since words and silence both drove him to deeper pain.

Yet despite his feelings about the people he came into contact with, he was certain that their presence sped up the healing process. "There is a sort of invisible blanket between the world and me. I find it hard to take in what anyone says.... It is so uninteresting. Yet I want the others to be about me. I dread the moments when the house is empty. If only they would talk to one another and not to me."

Eventually Lewis began to sense the daylight at the end of the tunnel of grief over losing his beloved wife. He wrote about not being tormented any longer by the mental image of her. As his memories of her opened up to brighter, less painful rumination, his openness to the love and peace of God increased as well. "I have gradually been coming to feel that the door is no longer shut and bolted."[15]

When the deepest hurt has shut you in, you can scream and kick against the walls, or you can fight your way forward, hoping in God like a shipwrecked sailor clinging to a life preserver in a raging ocean. If you can fight for joy, you will find yourself eventually standing at the open door, on the far side of grief and in the warmth and peace of the joy of the Lord.

Maybe you see no foothold in your fight for joy. Maybe you have no idea where to begin. Maybe life is so overwhelming and the darkness so great that you have little desire even to get out of bed in the morning. The good news is that you don't have to get to God; he can get to *you*. He's near you already, as he promised: "The LORD is close to the brokenhearted; he rescues those whose spirits are crushed."[16]

Learning to Forgive

On August 6, 1945, the United States dropped the first nuclear bomb on Hiroshima in an effort to bring World War II to an end. Tsutomu Yamaguchi was in Hiroshima on business that day and miraculously survived the blast, escaping with terrible burns over most of his body and a bare understanding of what had occurred. After his release from treatment, he returned to his hometown of Nagasaki. Two days after his arrival, on August 9, the United States dropped the second nuclear bomb on Nagasaki... and Mr. Yamaguchi. According to Japanese officials, he is the only individual officially acknowledged to have survived two nuclear bomb blasts. He was at ground zero of both these events, and despite exposure to devastating radiation (twice!), he managed to live past his ninety-third birthday.

Do you think he ever wondered why he was the one who got nuked twice? Do you think he harbored some bitterness? He certainly had cause!

We've already explored many aspects of how we move forward when we are torn. But the most important practical topic still remains. You see, through my counseling with individuals and through my own personal struggles, I have become convinced that a lack of forgiveness is the number-one obstacle to our healing and our joy. Our anger and unforgiveness may be directed toward God or people or often both. Yet if we don't deal with them, we'll never really heal.

When we are hurt, it is normal to channel our energy to the person or persons who did it. We want someone to be held responsible. We want the other to feel some of what we've felt, even if we know deep down we should move toward forgiveness. We're torn. And we often don't realize that the deeper wound is not the obvious one but the kind of wound that is healed only with forgiveness. If we are serious about healing and putting the pieces of our lives back together, then we have to address the issue of forgiveness.

> A lack of forgiveness is the number-one obstacle to our healing and our joy.

LEARNING FORGIVENESS

Back in 2004 a horrific YouTube video went viral. It was a video of a young man (later identified as Nicholas Berg), a civilian in Iraq, who was kidnapped by Islamic extremists. His captors put him on camera and decapitated him with a dull knife. I wanted to throw up when I watched the video, not realizing what I was going to see. The CIA later confirmed that the orchestrator of Berg's murder was Abu Musab al-Zarqawi, a major leader in al-Qaeda. His voice was heard on the tape, and he held the blunt knife that decapitated Nicholas Berg.

In 2006 al-Zarqawi himself was killed. At the time some reporters interviewed Michael Berg, Nicholas's dad. They wanted to know, "After the death of your son, how do you feel about his murderer's death?" They were blown away by the man's response.

Michael Berg began to talk about the fact that, six months after his son died, he had realized that a thirst for revenge was going to kill him. Anger was hijacking him. It was taking him places he didn't want to go. He was becoming a vindictive and bitter person. But he received a catalog in the mail from a Christian university that had a course on forgiveness. He took that course and began working through his pain. He said it took him about six months of processing. Long before al-Zarqawi was killed, Michael came to a place where he had already forgiven the terrorist. He told the reporters, "I don't rejoice today. I'm not celebrating today because he's now dead and something is out of my life that was there. I've come to a place where I've surrendered this; where I have given it to God."[1] He had come to a place of forgiveness.

As you can imagine, some people were outraged about this, begrudging Michael his arrival at a place of forgiveness. But Canadian musician Peter Katz heard the interview on the radio and was blown away by the grace and forgiveness in Berg's heart toward someone who had murdered his son. The musician pulled his car over and wrote a song called "Forgiveness." He dedicated the song to Michael and talked about him and his life.[2]

> You may want retaliation, you may want with everything within you to get even, but none of that will bring peace and justice into your life.

You may want retaliation, you may want with everything within you to get even, but the reality is that none of that will bring peace and justice into your life. Vigilante justice won't satisfy. That's why God says again and again in the Bible that vengeance is his.[3] "You trust me," God is saying. "I'll work it out. I'll take care of it. I will deal with the retaliation issues."

I'm not saying there is no place for justice or for military or police intervention. I'm talking about taking justice into your own hands or storing it up in your heart in a way that is harmful and destructive. There can be serious consequences to vigilante justice. Unchecked anger ratchets up and up; it never goes anywhere good. The more it expands, the more dangerous it gets.

THE TIME IS NOW

Jesus gave us some challenges to deal with the anger that may be welling up inside us. He said, "If you are presenting a sacrifice at the altar in the Temple and you suddenly remember that someone has something against you, leave your sacrifice there at the altar. Go and be reconciled to that person. Then come and offer your sacrifice to God."[4] People would often travel as much as eighty miles to get to the temple to present their sacrifice at the altar. Jesus was therefore saying, "You just traveled a whole week to get there. You finally get there, and you get up to the altar, and you are going to present your sacrifice. Then you remember not just that you are mad at somebody else but that somebody has a problem with you. What are you supposed to do?" Jesus said to leave. Walk for a day or two or a week. Go work it out, and then come back.

That's how important it is for us to try to make peace with others we're in conflict with.

You may have longed for an excuse to leave church in the middle of a service. Well, here's your proof text! Jesus is saying that when you are at church and you realize, "Man,

I have major issues with somebody" or, "Somebody has major issues with me," you had better commit to making it right as soon as possible. Don't delay for anything. Forgiveness is that important.

THE GIFT THAT GIVES

All of this is way easier to say than to do. When life throws you a curve ball that smacks you right in the gut and leaves you breathless, it is easy to hold on to bitterness and anger.

My friends Eric and Jayne discovered this.

They were driving home from work a few years ago on what seemed like a normal evening. Then, two blocks from home, they came across an accident scene, with emergency vehicles parked everywhere.

"It was like a scene from the movies," Jayne reflected. "The lights. The ambulances. The police cars. The yellow caution tape."

Jayne had a feeling that overwhelmed her motherly instincts. It was one of those feelings that words can't do justice to, that can't be articulated. But she and Eric couldn't tell what had happened at the scene, so they kept going.

When they got home, Jayne jumped out of her car, and as quick as her tired feet could move, she headed into the house. Immediately she asked the friends who were staying with them, "Where's Paul?" Paul was her sixteen-year-old son.

The response from her friends was innocent and direct: "We haven't seen him."

Without a pause Jayne turned to Eric and said, "Go find Paul."

Eric didn't need to hear any more. He knew what she was thinking. He headed out of the house and back to the yellow caution tape two blocks away.

Jayne sat and waited. The minutes slowly ticked by. Every thought you could possibly imagine raced through her mind. She thought that maybe Paul was at a friend's house or

A police officer walked into the house. He simply said, "Are you Jayne? Your son is dead."

that he was caught on the other side of the caution tape, unable to get home. She even thought that he might have been hurt, and she was planning on a trip to the hospital.

Then a quiet voice whispered to her. She knew.

What was moving at mach speed within her mind came to a stop when the front door opened and a police officer walked into the house. He simply asked, "Are you Jayne?" She didn't need to hear any more. She didn't want to hear any more. This was every parent's worst nightmare come to life. The cop continued, as she knew he would, "Your son is dead."

She collapsed on the floor. One of her most precious possessions had been ripped from her grasp. No option to protect him. No good-bye. No hug. No "I love you." Paul had been forcibly removed from his loving mother's arms.

As she learned later, the accident was the result of a tragic set of circumstances. Paul had been riding home on his bike. Meanwhile, another young man about his age, Tommy, newly in possession of a driver's license, was driving some friends home. He was hoping not to miss his ten o'clock curfew. Tommy simply didn't see Paul.

Over the following days, Paul's memory consumed every conversation. Tears blurred the eyes of all who knew and loved him. Rage loomed as everyone tried to understand the all-encompassing *why*. Why Paul? Why did the other teenager's parents allow him to drive with so little experience? Why was this boy paying attention to everything else going on around him in the car and not on the life right outside his windshield?

Someone behind Jayne whispered, "That's him." This was the first time she'd laid eyes on the boy who had taken her son's life.

Seven days went by, filled with emotional napalm.

Right after the funeral, Jayne found herself standing in the middle of a mob of well-intentioned people. Person after person walked up to Jayne to express words of encouragement and condolence. She was overwhelmed by the love and support of so many people, yet she felt empty at the same time.

Then Jayne looked up to see a boy coming toward her, his parents gently pushing him forward in an agonizing walk of uncertainty. His lip was quivering as he tried to hold himself together. Then someone behind Jayne leaned over to her and whispered, "That's him. That's Tommy."

Jayne had never met him, never talked to him, never even seen a picture of him. This was the first time she'd laid eyes on the boy who had taken her son's life. Jayne had only a moment to decide what to do, how to react, what to say. The anger that had loomed underneath the surface all week desperately desired to explode onto the teenage boy standing in front of her.

She prayed a simple prayer. "What do I do, Lord? What do I do?"

Without a pause she heard God say one simple word: forgive.

Forgive is a verb. It's an action. It requires you not just to say the words but to live them out. So many good-hearted people say they forgive, yet they continue to verbally berate individuals who have hurt them. People say they forgive yet hold on to grudges that implant themselves into the framework of their lives. Jayne knew this was a bridge she had to cross.

Tommy, in despair, looked up at Jayne and said, "I'm sorry."

Jayne stared at this boy. At that moment everything around her was blocked out. She was overwhelmed by how much he looked like her son. With God's command still ringing in her head, she gently said to Tommy, "If you could take back that day, you would."

With those words said, she pulled a ring out of her pocket. It was Paul's promise ring, a gift she had given him years ago. She'd had it with her all week, receiving comfort from it as she began to navigate life without Paul. She handed the ring to Tommy. The next minutes became a blur as she extended the greatest gift she could give to this devastated boy: forgiveness.

Almost a year later Jayne found herself looking ahead to the anniversary of her son's death. What would you do in that situation? Jayne continued what God had set in motion after the funeral. She invited a houseful of Paul's friends over to celebrate his life. She then took a moment to share the message of Christ's radical grace. That night, in her living room, eighteen of Paul's friends accepted Christ as their Lord and Savior, as their leader, forgiver, and friend. Among those who made that life-changing decision was Tommy.

Through a horrific tragedy, a life was given. Through amazing forgiveness, a life was saved.

Now, I can't promise that forgiveness will always have the same miraculous results as it did with Jayne and Tommy. The supernatural work inside the heart of one who forgives is something we can depend on. But sometimes the one who needs to be forgiven isn't nearly so ready to receive it as Tommy was.

The Bible says, "If it is possible, as far as it depends on you, live at peace with everyone."[5] The challenge is that it doesn't completely depend on you. It also depends on the other person. I've apologized to people I've wronged and sought forgiveness. Most of the time that has gone well, but a few times the other person has refused to accept my apology or extend forgiveness. You can control only what you can control.

Forgiveness doesn't mean all is now well. Forgiveness doesn't mean there are no consequences for what others have done. Forgiveness doesn't mean the legal system can't play its hand. Forgiveness means that at the end of the day, you forfeit your personal right to get even. You say, "I give you to the sovereign God, who rules over all."

> If you continue to go down the road of anger, the issue will continue to heat up, and there will be consequences.

After telling his followers to drop their sacrifices at the altar, if necessary to seek forgiveness, Jesus went on to say, "When you are on the way to court with your adversary, settle your differences quickly." He's saying we need to do this quickly, otherwise "your accuser may hand you over to the judge, who will hand you over to an officer, and you will be thrown into prison. And if that happens, you surely won't be free again until you have paid the last penny."[6] Jesus was not trying to give legal advice here. He was using this as an illustration. If you continue to go down the road of anger, if you don't allow yourself to move to a place where you can make peace, the issue will continue to heat up, and there will be consequences.

THE REAL WOUND

Richard Moore of Northern Ireland was just ten years old when he was coming home and a young British soldier shot him in the face with a rubber bullet. Moore was blind from that moment. Throughout his life he wrestled with anger, bitterness, and rage toward the British and particularly toward that soldier.

Thirty years after the incident, he knew he needed to put it behind him. After lengthy research he was able to find the soldier who had shot him and to schedule a meeting. There, amid tears and regret, forgiveness was extended and received. Moore said, "After that, something peculiar and wonderful happened. Something inside me changed, something paradoxical. I began to realize that the gift of forgiveness I thought I was bestowing on the soldier who shot me was actually a gift from God to me. It didn't even matter whether the soldier wanted or needed forgiveness; the gift freed me, leaving me with a sense of serenity and blessedness.

"All through my boyhood my mother had wanted the impossible for me—that I would be given back my sight." He remembered waking up in the middle of the night as a kid, and his mom would be on her knees beside his bed pleading with God to restore his eyesight. He said, "When I met the soldier and forgave him, I believe my mother's prayers were answered. I was given a new vision, and my real wound, the one that needed healing more than my eyes, was healed."[7] The deeper wound, the real wound, had finally been healed.

> We'll find so much more freedom and so much more joy in our lives if we will let it go and forgive.

We can find healing from our wounds as well. I wonder how many of us in our frustration and anger toward others would find hope and healing if we could just step back long enough to realize that the person who hurt us, that person whom we may feel rage toward (and maybe he deserves our anger!), is still a person made in the image of God. That person still reflects the heavenly Father. We'll find so much more freedom and so much more joy in our lives if we will let it go and forgive.

Are there people you need to forgive? Is your anger toward someone else continuing to grow? Does bitterness have a foothold in your life? If so, don't let your unforgiveness hijack all the good stuff going on in your life.

Reflect on God's amazing grace and forgiveness to you. Then reach out to someone you need to forgive. Offer that forgiveness, realizing that the most important part of the process is not how the other person reacts but what goes on inside your own heart.

When we were in desperate need, God sent Jesus here to meet that need. When others are in desperate need, we can be the living evidence of the God of the new creation for others.

Conclusion

As challenging and overwhelming as the *why* questions are in our lives, we've seen that the Bible points us to a more fundamental and important question: *who*. Who will we trust? Who will we hang on to in the storms of life? Again and again we are challenged to trust God, to cling to him, to find refuge in him. He is good, and he is working his plan even when we can't see it. All of this often requires us to grow up in our faith and reframe our expectations of God and others. We realize that the world is about God and his glory more than it is about us and our comfort. We learn to worship and take the risk of courageous trust.

After we move beyond being stuck in the endless cycle of *why* questions and settle the *who* question, we long to know *how* we can move forward, putting the pieces back together. We've seen that this is not a road to be walked alone but one to be shared with others as we wait for God, fight for joy, learn to forgive, and live in God's grace each moment. We've considered many practical things involved in experiencing God in the tough seasons and moving forward with hope and healing.

The world is about God and his glory more than it is about us and our comfort.

If anyone could have been paralyzed by the *why* questions concerning his own childhood or the suffering in our torn world, it would be my friend Wess Stafford, president of Compassion International, a child relief organization. He grew up in the Ivory Coast of Africa, in the village of Nielle. He was the son of Baptist missionaries. He talks of sleeping on a cot at night and hearing drums in the distance. The drums would sometimes announce the arrival of strangers or mark the celebration of a festival, but they also would sound out the eulogy of kids who had died from malaria or measles or snakebites. Wess lay on his cot and wept for them when the drum announced their deaths. These people were not statistics for him but his friends.

He recalls one traumatic experience when a snake bit one of his best friends as they played. Everyone knew there was no time to get help, and Wess held him in his arms as he died. He keeps a picture in his office of his childhood friends from the village. Most of them died before they were eighteen.

Wess also has a bell that reminds him of the one that would ring when he attended an abusive boarding school abroad. The bell would ring, and the teachers would read a list of the kids who had been "bad." Then they would endure horrible physical and verbal abuse. At one point he estimated that he'd been beaten an average of seventeen times a week. Wess thought this was normal. The world was cruel, and kids paid the price.

He had every right to retreat within himself and his pain, but instead he joined in with the suffering of others to make a difference. He served as a field officer with Compassion and eventually with the corporate office before becoming president. There is no one like Wess. He's brilliant, with a PhD in philosophy from Michigan State University, but he shuns traditional top-down leadership models and takes the role of a servant to the organization he leads and the people he helps. He says, "People have a couple [of] basic needs beyond food and shelter. Everyone longs to be known and loved." And Wess makes everyone around him feel that both of those needs are valued.

As I walked with him in a slum area in Ecuador, I was so thankful that Wess allowed God to use his pain and suffering to help others. On our trip he was often found kneeling to be eye level with the kids he loves so much. You sense he leads Compassion to leverage the greatest influence, but he'd really just love to work directly with the kids himself.

His care for the children of the world is contagious. Now Compassion is serving people in more than twenty-five countries and is constantly ranked at the highest level of nonprofit organizations for both fiscal responsibility and effectiveness. Wess has been torn, but he's trusting God and serving others out of that pain and bringing hope to the world. I'm so thankful.

KEEP MOVING

We've seen that God knows you and loves you. He knows what your future will be like, and he wants you to have hope in it, even now when all hope seems lost. When your life is shattered in some painful way, every moment thereafter can feel like an aftershock. Your soul will ache for some stability, some security. Find this security in Jesus. In John 15:4, Jesus says, "Remain in me, and I will remain in you. For a branch cannot produce fruit if it is severed from the vine, and you cannot be fruitful unless you remain in me." Plant yourself firmly in Jesus, and keep trusting him.

Consider this: approximately 70 percent of a human being is made up of water. Water is the greatest life source we have. You can go weeks without food, but without water you have at most a few days to live. Yet for all the life-giving effects of water, if it goes stagnant, it has devastating effects. Stagnant water is a breeding ground for mosquitoes, the main carriers of malaria and dengue fever. In addition, stagnant water contains many kinds of harmful, even deadly, bacteria and parasites.

So how does water become stagnant? Simply put, it stops flowing. There's no movement.

Whatever you do, don't go stagnant in your life. Pain desires for you to hunker down and go into self-preservation mode. Pain wants you to cover up and hide. Whatever you do, don't do that! Fight the urge. Keep moving, keep growing, keep praying, keep screaming, keep crying, keep asking, and keep searching.

A wise man once compared life to a wheelbarrow. If you try to turn a loaded wheelbarrow while it's stationary, it will tip over. But if you get that same wheelbarrow moving, you can easily steer it in any direction.

> Whatever you do, don't go stagnant in your life. Keep moving, keep growing, keep praying, keep screaming, and keep searching.

Keep moving, and allow God to steer your life. It may sound like a cheap Sunday school cop-out to suggest that a hurting person read his Bible, pray, and stay connected to the church community. But we don't have to invent new steps to get closer to God and further into healing. The "old" stuff works just fine, if we will actually do it.

Maybe you can get creative in how you approach these things. Print out Bible verses that are especially meaningful in this time, and tape them to your dashboard, your computer, your bathroom mirror, whatever. Get out of the house, and meet friends in the park or at the bowling alley. Create new memories with old friends, a way to start forging ahead in your recovery. Ask for prayer. The old ways still work, but feel free to freshen them up. Perhaps even brainstorming how to do this can get your mind focused on positive things.

ALL THINGS NEW

We receive this great news from God's Word: "Behold, I am making all things new."[1] This is a promise, of course. It looks toward the future. But the word *behold* implies that we are seeing it, which in turn implies that we are *looking* for it. You can't behold Jesus making all things new if you have retreated into yourself and avoided prayer, God's Word, and fellowship with others.

> Whatever you are going through, believe this: God can and will use it both to bring good into your life and to bring his glory into the world.

Another great promise from Scripture (one we have already looked at) is this: "God causes everything to work together for the good of those who love God and are called according to his purpose for them."[2] Whatever you are going through, believe this: God can and will use it both to bring good into your life and to bring his glory into the world. Fresh brokenness becomes a fresh start. Different difficulties become different perspectives. New setbacks become new opportunities. Deep pains become deep devotions to the Savior. Even our scars and wounds can be used in our healing if we will remember the mortal wounds Christ received for us.

Psalm 23 may be the most famous passage in all the Bible (next to John 3:16, I suppose). And for good reason. But maybe we've dulled the comfort it holds by putting it on sweatshirts and coffee mugs. This psalm of David reveals a sorrowful heart but a hopeful one too. In verse 4 we find this sobering reminder:

> Even though I walk through the valley of the
>   shadow of death,
>   I will fear no evil,
> for you are with me;
>   your rod and your staff,
>   they comfort me.[3]

When David says, "the valley of the shadow of death," he means it. He is not using hyperbole. People wanted him dead—King Saul among them. He was a marked man. David knew what it meant to enter into the depression of pain, to despair of his own life. Nevertheless, because he knew his life had been charted before time even began by the God who loves him eternally, he could take heart, reject fear, and find comfort in the leading of the Lord.

David was a man who committed great sins, including adultery and murder. He was a man who knew great grief, having lost a child. He was a man who knew great emotional pain, having felt plenty of times as though God had abandoned him. And he also knew what it felt like to be abandoned, threatened, challenged, and hated by others. And yet this is how he ends Psalm 23:

> Surely goodness and mercy shall follow me
> all the days of my life,
> and I shall dwell in the house of the LORD
> forever.[4]

If you truly trust in Jesus Christ for your salvation, even with only a small amount of faith, the Lord will blaze the path before you like a shepherd, and goodness and mercy will follow you for the rest of your days.

You may be torn right now. But *look*! He is making all things new.

STUDY GUIDE

In part 2 of *Torn*, the first advice I give about managing your personal suffering is to "share the struggle." Don't face your problems alone. Let others know what is going on, and accept their help.

Because I believe so strongly that the Christian life is a shared activity, I couldn't publish this book without including a study guide. Sure, you'd get some benefit if you merely read the book by yourself. But if you join with a few friends who are themselves torn, and discuss the issues together, well, you'll get *so much more* out of the book! And you'll go so much farther down the road to recovery.

When you get together with your group members, bring a copy of *Torn*, a Bible, and a determination to be absolutely honest about what you're going through. Jesus promises to be present whenever two or three are gathered in his name, and so you can be confident that he will be there with your group. In fact, he will be at work inside each of you, mending the torn places in your hearts.

—Jud Wilhite

SESSION 1

Torn Apart

Read the introduction and chapter 1 of *Torn*.

OPENING THOUGHTS

1. How are you torn right now? Tell the story.

2. What are you hoping to get out of reading and discussing this book?

CHAPTER REVIEW

3. What *why* questions are you asking about your torn experience?

4. Chapter 1 says, "The danger with *why* questions is that they lead to a dark, confusing, frustrating, lonely, disconnected place.... *Why* keeps you in the past and blocks you from moving forward." How have you found this to be true in your life?

5. Would you agree with Jud that it's better to ask *who* rather than *why*? That is, to trust God rather than to seek explanations for suffering? Explain your answer.

6. How easy or hard are you finding it to trust God right now, despite your suffering? What do you think it will take for you to trust God more?

7. What *how* questions do you have? In other words, in what areas do you see yourself needing practical help as you deal with being torn?

PERSONAL APPLICATION

Like Chris Trethewey in chapter 1, write a letter to God, telling him about your struggle and confusion. Be absolutely honest with him. Express your hurt, but also express your trust in him to the extent that you can.

If you're comfortable with doing so, read this letter to your *Torn* discussion group.

SESSION 2

Reframing Your Expectations

Read chapter 2 of *Torn*.

OPENING THOUGHTS

1. What are you struggling with when it comes to adjusting to the changes brought about by your torn experience?

CHAPTER REVIEW

2. How does the new *now* look different from the old *then* for you?

3. How is yearning for the past holding you back from moving more effectively into the future?

4. What do you think about the author's idea that we should look at the people, things, and experiences in our lives as loaners from God, not as possessions we can expect to keep? Reasonable or not?

5. If you were to adopt the loaner outlook, how might it help you?

6. What does it take for us to get to the place where we can say to God—as Jesus did in the Garden of Gethsemane—"I want your will to be done, not mine" (Mark 14:36)?

PERSONAL APPLICATION

Using a piece of paper, list in the left-hand column your expectations of God and faith that have been affected by your experience of suffering. List in the right-hand column how you may need to adjust each of those expectations.

Share your list with your fellow group members, and receive their advice and encouragement.

SESSION 3

Life Interrupted

Read chapter 3 of *Torn*.

OPENING THOUGHTS

1. How do you most relate personally to the biblical character Job?

CHAPTER REVIEW

2. In the opening chapters of Job, what do the behind-the-scenes negotiations between God and Satan reveal about the nature of human suffering? What questions do they leave unanswered?

3. What is the difference between cursing God and verbalizing your hurt to him honestly?

4. What things in nature or human experience most powerfully reveal to you the absolute authority of God?

5. How does the book of Job illustrate the "who not why" principle?

6. Although Job was wonderfully rewarded before death, many of us have to wait until heaven for our pain to be replaced with pleasure. Are you comfortable with waiting for pie in the sky, or do you just want to eat it now?

7. Chapter 3 says, "Trusting God when torn is the normative experience of believers throughout the Bible. It's okay if you can't figure out why; just keep hanging on to the God who is hanging on to you." How are you doing at hanging on?

PERSONAL APPLICATION

When Job was in a crisis, he worshiped God. Follow his lead. Worship God with your fellow *Torn* group members. Sing worship songs, praise God in prayer, or do whatever else your group agrees on to worship together.

Courageous Trust

Read chapter 4 of *Torn.*

OPENING THOUGHTS

1. In the midst of your suffering, have you ever doubted God's love for you? If your answer is yes, describe what was going through your mind.

CHAPTER REVIEW

2. How can it be true that God loves us if he allows terrible things to happen to us?

3. How does suffering tend to blind us to God's love?

4. Do you think of God as more detached from your feelings of pain or as more sympathetic to them? Why?

5. What makes the resurrection of Christ a strong proof of God's love for us?

6. How would your reaction to your suffering be different if you were not a believer in Jesus Christ?

PERSONAL APPLICATION

Courageous trust is answering the question, "Can the dead live again?" with an emphatic, "Yes, and by faith *I will.*" So are you ready to declare your trust in the all-powerful, all-loving God who promises ultimate redemption? If so, write on a piece of paper what you want to say to God. If you have never trusted in Christ for salvation, do that now. Or if you need to declare your trust in God to bring provisional healing in this life and final healing in the life to come, then do that.

Share what you have written with your group.

Share the Struggle

Read chapter 5 of *Torn*.

OPENING THOUGHTS

1. Do you feel alone in dealing with your suffering and problems? Or do you feel that you have a team standing with you? If you are alone, why is that?

CHAPTER REVIEW

2. When you are hurting, are you more likely to seek out the company of others, or do you retreat into yourself? Why?

3. What makes it hard to be honest and open with others about our suffering? What are the advantages if we will make the attempt?

4. How do you feel when others are honest and open with you about their suffering?

5. In what ways have you been a minister of God's grace and comfort to others who were hurting?

6. How would you like fellow believers to help you in your suffering right now?

PERSONAL APPLICATION

A culture of grace is a group—large or small—where people are encouraged to share what they are really going through and are freely accepted. With your *Torn* group, discuss the cultures of grace you have available to help you in your times of trouble. (Hopefully your *Torn* group is itself a culture of grace!) Also discuss how you could possibly help to create a new culture of grace.

Reach out for help and give help, in God's grace.

SESSION 6

Check Your Assumptions

Read chapter 6 of *Torn*.

Opening Thoughts

1. Do you ever worry that your suffering is God's punishment for a specific sin you committed? If so, describe what goes through your mind at those times.

Chapter Review

2. Biblically, what are the arguments against the "God is punishing you" assumption about suffering?

3. What unnecessary pain can this assumption cause?

4. Have others told you that you need to have more faith or to confess sin in order to be free of your suffering? Describe what you've heard.

5. What's wrong with the "you just need more faith" assumption?

6. Describe what you see as the differences between healthy guilt and unhealthy guilt.

PERSONAL APPLICATION

If you're dealing with unhealthy guilt over some sin you committed in the past, do what Jud told one of his guilt-ridden church members to do: read Psalm 51, and confess your sin to God one more time. You may also want to confess this sin to your *Torn* group (James 5:16). And then don't ever confess that sin again.

If you're tempted later to feel condemned for that sin, claim Bible promises such as the following:

- "He has removed our sins as far from us as the east is from the west." (Psalm 103:12)
- "There is no condemnation for those who belong to Christ Jesus." (Romans 8:1)
- "If we confess our sins to him, he is faithful and just to forgive us our sins and to cleanse us from all wickedness." (1 John 1:9)

Waiting for God

Read chapter 7 of *Torn*.

OPENING THOUGHTS

1. Do you feel as if you are in a waiting room, waiting for your suffering to pass, waiting for God to act on your behalf? If so, what does that feel like?

   On a scale of 1 to 10, what is your impatience level, with 1 being "I can handle it" and 10 being "Get me out of here!"?

   1 2 3 4 5 6 7 8 9 10

CHAPTER REVIEW

2. Have you ever experienced a dark night of the soul, a time when God felt impossibly distant and depressingly silent? (Maybe you're going through one right now.) If so, describe it.

3. What can give you confidence that God is alive and active and still working for your good even when you don't see it?

4. How might God be using your dark night of the soul to mature your faith or prepare you for greater service to him?

5. What times in your past stand out as examples of God showing his faithfulness and blessing you? How can recalling these times encourage you in your present waiting period?

6. How can recalling Jesus's sacrificial death and victorious resurrection encourage you?

7. Do you ever feel ashamed because you are in a bad place and waiting for God to act? If so, how can you wait with more confidence and hope?

PERSONAL APPLICATION

Choose one or more of the following action steps to find comfort while you're waiting for God to alleviate your suffering. Share your choices with your group.

- If you are feeling isolated...reach out to a community who can share your life and hardships with you.
- If you need a chance to reflect on what is happening to you...spend time in solitude processing your hurts with God.
- If you feel that your experience is bottled up within you...let it out in words, music, or whatever other way comes most naturally to you.
- If you have lost someone dear to you... think of some act or ritual to memorialize the loss.
- If you need a reminder that God knows what you are going through...review stories of sufferers and God's words of comfort to them in Scripture.

SESSION 8

Fight for Joy

Read chapter 8 of *Torn*.

Opening Thoughts

1. Would you say that you are in the midst of depression right now? Have you ever been in a depression? If so, describe it.

Chapter Review

2. How have you seen people put pressure on other Christians to pretend that things are going well even if they are not? Have you ever put that kind of pressure on yourself?

3. How do you feel about Christians getting medical treatment for depression—okay or not?

4. If you are experiencing depression, how do you think God might be using it to prepare you for a greater blessing?

5. If you are experiencing depression, how hopeful are you that God will bring it to an end? What are you doing to fight for joy?

PERSONAL APPLICATION

Choose one or more new actions that will be the right moves in your fight for joy.

- See a doctor, and follow his or her recommendations.
- Eat better.
- Exercise more.
- Adopt a new hobby or a new pet.
- Pray more.
- Adjust your attitude and mental focus.
- Other: _____

SESSION 9

Learning to Forgive

Read chapter 9 and the conclusion of *Torn*.

OPENING THOUGHTS

1. In what way is anger toward another person—
   or toward God—a part of your present torn
   experience?

CHAPTER REVIEW

2. Chapter 9 says, "A lack of forgiveness is the
   number-one obstacle to our healing and our joy."
   Do you agree or disagree? Why?

3. Describe a time when you forgave someone
   who had hurt you. Or describe a time when
   you were the one who received forgiveness.
   What did you learn about forgiveness from the
   experience?

4. What is wrong with seeking revenge when someone has hurt us?

5. What are the costs of holding on to bitterness and anger?

6. What are the benefits of forgiving?

7. How can God's forgiveness of you motivate your forgiveness of others?

PERSONAL APPLICATION

Do you need to forgive someone? If so, get your group members' help in planning how you will do that. Then don't delay. Forgive from your heart, and move on toward recovery.

WRAP-UP

8. What have you gained from reading and discussing *Torn* with the group?

9. How do you plan to use the fundamental spiritual disciplines of praying, reading God's Word, and

spending time with fellow believers to look for how God is "making all things new" for you (Revelation 21:5, ESV)?

10. How are you already seeing signs of God healing you where you are torn?

ACKNOWLEDGMENTS

No author is an island, and I'm thankful for the many who played a role in helping me shape the ideas and thoughts of this book: Drew Bodine, Justin Jackson, Michael Murphy, Chris Trethewey, Jared Wilson, and too many others to name who indirectly influenced the direction.

Thanks to those who put themselves out there and shared their stories. I know it is a little unsettling, but you'll bring hope to so many, as you have to me.

Huge thanks to the editorial team at WaterBrook Multnomah for putting up with me and keeping me on track: Dave Kopp and Eric Stanford.

Chris Ferebee with Yates & Yates did a fantastic job, as usual, and I'm grateful for your friendship.

Large portions of this book were drafted while listening to Jack's Mannequin. Edits were done to Wes Montgomery and a touch of the *Glee* Christmas album. I know, it's an eclectic mix. Thanks for the inspiration.

I'm grateful to Central Christian Church for embodying what it means to accept people where they are and to help them grow. Thanks for inspiring me to trust God no matter what and for "being the church" to a hurting world.

Acknowledgments

Thanks to Eugena Kelting for being the awesome air traffic controller for my life and for serving God with your whole heart. And thanks to the staff and volunteers at Central for your loyalty, faith, and passionate commitment to radical grace, radical alignment, and church health.

Thanks to Lori, Emma, Ethan, and Roxy for unconditional love, a safe haven to call home, lots of laughs, and consistent encouragement. I love you!

Notes

Introduction

1. "Very Old Friends," *The Lord of the Rings: The Fellowship of the Ring*, DVD, directed by Peter Jackson (Los Angeles: New Line Cinema, 2001).
2. Job 23:2, MSG.
3. Bart Ehrman, quoted in Stanley Fish, "Suffering, Evil and the Existence of God," *New York Times*, November 4, 2007, http://opinionator.blogs.nytimes .com/2007/11/04/suffering-evil-and-the-existence -of-god.

Chapter 1

1. See "Membership—Join Bloody Knuckles," World Bloody Knuckles Association, www.bloodyknuckles .org/index.htm.
2. Isaiah 46:9–10.
3. Job 38:4–39:30.
4. Romans 11:36.
5. Luke 12:4–5.
6. Romans 5:3–4.

Chapter 2

1. Camerin Courtney, "Blessed Disillusionment," Kyria Online, 2005, www.kyria.com/topics/hottopics/thesinglelife/mind50330.html?start=1.

2. 2 Corinthians 1:5.

3. Job 1:21.

4. Augustine, *City of God,* trans. Henry Bettenson (New York: Penguin, 1972), 18, 20.

5. James 1:17.

6. Mark 14:36.

7. Mark 15:34; Luke 23:46.

8. Philip Yancey, *Disappointment with God: Three Questions No One Asks Aloud* (Carmel, NY: Guideposts, 1988), 245–46.

Chapter 3

1. Scott Rigsby, quoted in "The Scott Rigsby Story: Unthinkable," www.scottrigsby.com.

2. Job 1:1.

3. Ezekiel 14:14, 20.

4. Job 1:3.

5. Matthew 25:41.

6. Job 1:8.

7. Job 1:9–11.

8. Job 1:12.

9. Job 1:12.

10. Job 1:20.

11. Job 1:20.

12. Job 38:1.

13. Job 38:2.

14. Job 38:3.

15. Job 38:31.

16. Richard Swenson, *More than Meets the Eye: Fascinating Glimpses of God's Power and Design* (Colorado Springs: NavPress, 2000), 149.

17. Job 42:10, 12–13.

18. Job 42:16–17.

19. Job 13:15, ESV.

Chapter 4

1. Brennan Manning, *Ruthless Trust: The Ragamuffin's Path to God* (San Francisco: HarperCollins, 2002), 3–4.

2. Ephesians 2:14, ESV.

3. Psalm 34:18; Jeremiah 29:11; Zechariah 2:8; 1 Peter 5:7; Psalm 103:17; Lamentations 3:22.

4. Tony Snow, "Cancer's Unexpected Blessings," Christianity Today Online, July 20, 2007, www.christianitytoday.com/ct/2007/july/25 .30.html.

5. Matthew 10:29–31.

6. John 16:33.

206

Notes

7. D. A. Carson, *How Long, O Lord? Reflections on Suffering and Evil* (Grand Rapids, MI: Baker, 1990), 243.

8. 1 Corinthians 13:8.

9. *The Princess Bride,* directed by Rob Reiner (Beverly Hills: Act III Communications, 1987).

10. John 11:35.

11. John 16:33.

12. Job 14:14.

13. 1 Peter 1:8.

14. Job 19:25–27.

15. Matthew 5:3–12, NIV.

16. C. S. Lewis, *Mere Christianity* (New York: Macmillan, 1952), 118–21.

17. Ephesians 1:10, NASB.

18. Job 16:21.

Chapter 5

1. Romans 12:15; Galatians 6:2; 1 Corinthians 12:26; 2 Corinthians 1:4–7.

2. Bono, quoted in "One (U2 Song)," Wikipedia, http://en.wikipedia.org/wiki/One_(U2_song)#cite_ref-11.

3. John 17:20–23.

4. Romans 5:8.

5. Dietrich Bonhoeffer, *Life Together* (San Francisco: Harper & Row, 1954), 23.

6. Genesis 3:7–11.

7. Genesis 3:21.

Chapter 6

1. John 9:2–3.

2. John 8:32.

3. C. S. Lewis, *A Grief Observed* (New York: Harper-Collins, 1961), 15.

4. *Super Size Me: A Film of Epic Portions,* directed by Morgan Spurlock (New York: Kathbur Pictures, 2004).

5. Luke 13:4–5.

6. Acts 17:31; 2 Timothy 4:1, ESV.

7. 2 Peter 3:9, ESV.

8. 1 Thessalonians 5:9, ESV.

9. Psalm 103:12.

10. Romans 8:1.

Chapter 7

1. Aron Ralston, quoted in "Then & Now: Aron Ralston," CNN, June 19, 2005, www.cnn.com/2005/US/04/04/cnn25.tan.ralston/index.html.

2. Psalm 69:1–3.

3. Psalm 69:14–15, 34.

4. Andrew Murray, *Waiting on God!* (New York: Revell, 1896), 47.

5. Paul Reber, "What Is the Memory Capacity of the Human Brain?" *Scientific American Mind,* May 2010, www.scientificamerican .com/article.cfm?id=what-is-the-memory -capacity.

6. Deuteronomy 31:6; Joshua 1:5; Hebrews 13:5.

7. Earl Warren, quoted in Jim Newton, *Justice for All: Earl Warren and the Nation He Made* (New York: Penguin, 2007), 407.

8. Psalm 22:1.

9. Psalm 22:27–28, NIV.

10. Matthew 27:46.

11. Isaiah 53:5.

12. *The Edge,* directed by Lee Tamahori (Los Angeles: Twentieth Century Fox, 1997).

13. Psalm 25:3, ESV.

14. 1 Peter 4:16.

Chapter 8

1. See "What Is Depression?" All About Depression, www.allaboutdepression.com/gen_01.html.

2. Charles Spurgeon, quoted in John Piper, "Charles Spurgeon: Preaching Through Adversity," *Founders*

Journal, www.founders.org/journal/fj23/article1
.html.

3. Charles Spurgeon, quoted in Elizabeth Ruth
   Skoglund, *Bright Days, Dark Nights: With Charles
   Spurgeon in Triumph over Emotional Pain* (Grand
   Rapids, MI: Baker, 2000), 32–33.

4. Job 13:15, KJV.

5. Spurgeon, quoted in Piper, "Charles Spurgeon:
   Preaching Through Adversity."

6. Richard Winter, *The Roots of Sorrow: Reflections on
   Depression and Hope* (Wheaton, IL: Crossway,
   1986), 55.

7. Skoglund, *Bright Days, Dark Nights,* 31.

8. Proverbs 17:22, NKJV.

9. Jonah 4:1–9; Jeremiah 20:14–18; Psalm 42:3, 5, NIV.

10. 1 Kings 19:4, ESV.

11. 1 Kings 19:12; see *The ESV Study Bible* (Wheaton,
    IL: Crossway, 2008), 636.

12. Philippians 4:8.

13. Proverbs 4:23, NASB.

14. David Martyn Lloyd-Jones, *Spiritual Depression:
    Its Causes and Its Cure* (Grand Rapids: Eerdmans,
    1965), 210.

15. C. S. Lewis, *A Grief Observed* (New York: Harper-
    Collins, 1961), 3, 46.

16. Psalm 34:18.

Chapter 9

1. Michael Berg, quoted in audio interview, Peter Katz, www.peterkatz.org/audio/peterkatz_aih interview.mp3.

2. See Peter Katz, www.peterkatz.com/forgiveness .html.

3. Leviticus 19:18; Deuteronomy 32:35; Proverbs 24:29; Romans 12:17–19; 1 Thessalonians 5:15.

4. Matthew 5:23–24.

5. Romans 12:18, NIV.

6. Matthew 5:25–26.

7. Richard Moore, quoted in audio interview by Pat Coyle for Sacred Space, http://sacredspace.ie/ en/a-journey-in-forgiveness/.

Conclusion

1. Revelation 21:5, ESV.

2. Romans 8:28.

3. Psalm 23:4, ESV.

4. Psalm 23:6, ESV.

About the Author

Jud Wilhite is an author, speaker, and the senior pastor of Central Christian Church in Las Vegas, Nevada. More than nineteen thousand people attend its multiple campuses each weekend, along with a global community who attend online. Jud's books include *Throw It Down, Eyes Wide Open,* and *Uncensored Grace.* He and his wife, Lori, live in the Las Vegas area with their children and a slobbery bulldog named Roxy.

Discover the *real* you.

A travel guide through real spirituality from one incomplete person to another, *Eyes Wide Open* is a book of stories about following God in the messes of life, about broken pasts and our lifelong need for grace. It is a book about seeing ourselves and God with new eyes—eyes wide open to a God of love.

What happens in Las Vegas...

could change your life.

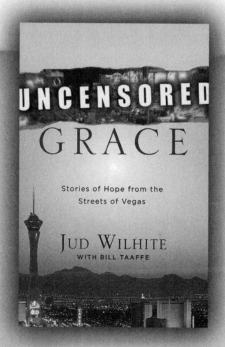

Behind the glitz and glam of Sin City, an amazing story is unfolding. It's a story of what can happen when Christians open their arms wide—really wide—in the name of Christ. *Uncensored Grace* introduces you to card players, exotic dancers, a flying Elvis, an American Idol contestant, and a beat cop turned hero, among others. Each has one thing in common—at their moment of extreme need they encounter an extraordinary God.

Previously published in hardcover as *Stripped: Uncensored Grace on the Streets of Vegas*.